THE EASY CAMP COOKBOOK

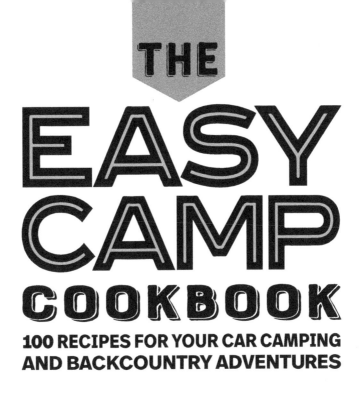

THE EASY CAMP COOKBOOK

100 RECIPES FOR YOUR CAR CAMPING AND BACKCOUNTRY ADVENTURES

AMELIA MAYER

ILLUSTRATIONS BY CLARE OWEN

ROCKRIDGE
PRESS

For general information on our other products and services or to obtain technical support, please contact our Customer Care Department within the United States at (866) 744-2665, or outside the United States at (510) 253-0500.

Rockridge Press publishes its books in a variety of electronic and print formats. Some content that appears in print may not be available in electronic books, and vice versa.

Interior and Cover Designer: Angela Navarra
Art Producer: Sue Bischofberger
Editor: Gurvinder Singh Gandu
Production Manager: Holly Haydash
Production Editor: Matthew Burnett

Illustration © 2020 Clare Owen

ISBN: Print 978-1-64739-030-3 | eBook 978-1-64739-031-0
R0

A huge thank you to my husband and kids,
who support my crazy ideas, and to my friends,
who so graciously helped me test recipes
to get them just right.

CONTENTS

INTRODUCTION

The food that you eat while camping or backpacking is usually unforgettable, for better or worse. After a long day outside or on the trail, food just tastes better than it does at home.

I grew up camping in Alaska both in a tent and in our remote, rustic family cabin. I still remember the 7UP cake in the Dutch oven and *the* best Thanksgiving dinner we ever had, cooked over a campfire.

Now that I have my own family, I find it crucial to be prepared for a hungry herd of five kids with meals that are easy to prep, cook, and serve. Simplicity is key while camping. However, that doesn't mean you have to settle for hot dogs and subpar freeze-dried foods on the trail.

This book is a compilation of my family's very favorite recipes that are (mostly) healthy, provide energy for fueling our adventures, and are simple to make.

You'll note that many of the recipes include some instructions on how to do some or all of the prep work at home. This will allow you to spend less time working at the campsite and more time relaxing and enjoying the outdoors.

I also hope you may be inspired to try a different method of cooking than you are used to. Cooking over a fire or using a Dutch oven takes a little practice, but the results are worth the extra effort. Camping is all about memories—and the food-related memories tend to be the ones that get passed on from generation to generation.

--- HOW TO USE THIS BOOK ---

This book is organized into two sections: car camping and backcountry camping. Neither type of camping is necessarily better than the other, but they do require distinctly different tools and methods. Car camping allows you to be a bit more liberal in the amount of gear you bring with you, whereas backcountry camping requires you to plan effectively since space is limited, so every single ounce counts.

I hope this book not only inspires your outdoor kitchen, but also challenges you to go a bit beyond your comfort zone. If your camping meals typically consist of food you just throw together as you pack the car, try something a little different (this book will give you lots of ideas!). If you are intimidated by backpacking or camping in general, let these simple meal ideas ease your mind.

The recipes are easy to make, delicious, and take the guesswork out of what is usually the most stressful part of camping—keeping everyone fed! Each recipe includes an icon that indicates the recommended cooking method for that particular dish as well as dietary labels that indicate whether a recipe is gluten-free, nut-free, dairy-free, vegan-friendly, or vegetarian-friendly.

COOKING METHOD ICONS

In this book, each recipe includes an icon that indicates my preferred cooking method for that particular dish, although you can usually modify cooking methods to fit your needs. Additionally, any recipes that feature the Prep Ahead icon include instructions for prepping and/or cooking at home to make things that much easier once you get to the campsite.

 CAMPFIRE: Foods cooked over a campfire are often done on a stick so they are easy to pull quickly out of the fire without burning yourself (or the food).

CAMP STOVE: The camp stove can be used either for car camping or for backcountry camping, though the kind of stove you use for each is very different. For car camping, a two-burner stove is great so you can have more than one dish going at a time. In the backcountry, a lightweight and portable stove is necessary for fast cooking and minimal carrying weight.

COAL: Coal cooking allows for even heat distribution, although it takes some time to get the coals heated to the perfect temperature.

DUTCH OVEN: Dutch oven cooking is some of my very favorite to do because it is forgiving and versatile. The Dutch oven can be used right on top of campfire coals while you cook with the lid on, and you can place coals on top of the lid. For easy cleanup, I recommend lining the Dutch oven with tinfoil.

 NO-COOK: No-cook foods are just that—you don't have to cook them, allowing you to get fueled up quickly. No-cook meals and snacks are perfect for backpacking and long days playing near the campsite.

PREP AHEAD: Some foods are just more difficult to cook while camping (example: bacon in bear country). I recommend making prep-ahead meals at home and placing them in resealable plastic freezer bags (I'd recommend going with a quality brand, as the cheaper alternatives don't work nearly as well), which you can then eat right out of.

SKILLET: I prefer a cast-iron skillet for car camping because it can be used both on a stove and on a fire, and is virtually indestructible. It is quite heavy though, so for backpacking, a skillet must be small and light and may be the only pan you bring along.

--- KNOW BEFORE YOU GO ---

Camping is hands down my favorite way to spend time with my family, mostly because it requires us to slow down and really focus on enjoying one another's company. However, it does require some planning and a little prepping to ensure that it ends up being a safe and pleasant experience. There's nothing worse than being unprepared, which can compromise the safety and enjoyment of the camping trip.

-- SAFETY --

The following is a list of safety tips that are imperative for campers to follow for a safe and fun camping experience.

ALWAYS HAVE A FIRST-AID KIT HANDY

Having a first-aid kit ready just in case could mean the difference between a pleasant experience and a trip to the ER. Although you can certainly put together your own (see the following list of suggested supplies), there are plenty of premade medical kits you can buy and then restock as needed.

If you're making your own kit, start with the following:

→ Alcohol-free cleansing wipes
→ Antihistamine cream or tablets
→ Antiseptic cream
→ Bandages

- $\rightarrow$ Disposable sterile gloves
- $\rightarrow$ Medical tape
- $\rightarrow$ Pain killers
- $\rightarrow$ Safety pins
- $\rightarrow$ Sterile gauze dressings in a variety of sizes
- $\rightarrow$ Tweezers

PRACTICE CAMPFIRE SAFETY

If you're building a campfire, be sure to do so in a designated area. This could be an existing fire ring or a ring of rocks you build yourself. Note that campfires aren't always allowed in certain areas, so always check the regulations of your campsite before you go.

Build your fire with natural items you find around your campsite, such as sticks and leaves, or fire starters you bring yourself. The most important part is to make sure your fire is completely out and cold to the touch before you leave it.

STORE YOUR FOOD PROPERLY

Never leave your food unattended. It should be locked in a car, a bear box (a sealed container specially made so that bears cannot smell the food inside), or hung at least 12 feet high if you are not sitting and actively prepping or eating your food. Because, well, bears.

STAY HYDRATED

Drink water consistently, even when you don't feel thirsty. At higher elevations or in hotter conditions, your body will need more water than you might be used to consuming. When you feel thirsty, you are already dehydrated. Be particularly mindful of hydration for small children. A good rule of thumb is to drink half your body weight in ounces of water each day.

USE INSECT AND SUN PROTECTION

Keep painful and damaging sunburns away by using a high SPF sunscreen and wearing long-sleeve shirts, pants, and hats. Those long layers, along with insect repellent, are also helpful in tick country. If you will be camping in areas with high populations of mosquitos, consider insect-protective hats for comfort. Insect repellant that contains DEET is the most effective, but should only be used when absolutely necessary. I like to use a more natural repellant, especially for my kids.

--- CHECK THE WEATHER FORECAST ---

Especially if you're camping in the mountains, weather conditions can change quickly. Check out the forecast before you go, and then monitor as necessary. Pack gear according to the forecast, but always bring extra layers just in case.

--- BE AWARE OF ALLERGIES ---

While camping, you may be exposed to plants that could cause allergies. Research where you will be camping to know what may be in the area and bring any appropriate allergy medication in your first-aid kit. It's also a good idea to consult with a physician ahead of time if you're concerned about any specific allergy triggers.

--- REMAIN ALERT ---

Camping is a great time to relax and have fun. However, it's important to pay attention to your body and surroundings. Be sure to get enough sleep.

--- BOIL OR FILTER DRINKING WATER ---

Any water that comes from a natural source (spring, river, lake, etc.) should be filtered or boiled for one minute at lower elevations and three minutes at higher elevations (6,562+ feet). This assures your safety as many of the most harmful microorganisms found in water are impossible to see. If boiling isn't possible, you should always carry a carbon or UV water filter, not only for drinking water, but also for things like washing/showering, cooking, washing dishes, rehydrating dried ingredients, etc.

LEAVE NO TRACE

No matter where you are camping, practicing "leave no trace" etiquette is absolutely crucial to minimizing impact on wildlife and ecosystems. The seven principles are outlined below.

1. Plan ahead and prepare. Be sure you know what you're getting yourself into before you go. Consider weather forecasts, terrain, regulations, abilities of the group, and anticipated food consumption. Being prepared helps avoid instances where campers need to be rescued, which potentially puts the lives of first responders in danger.

2. Travel and camp on durable surfaces. Stay on the trail and camp in designated spots to reduce scars on the landscape and unnecessary erosion.

3. Dispose of waste properly. Pack it in, pack it out.

4. Leave what you find. Despite how cool that rock or flower is, leave it behind for someone else to enjoy in its natural location.

5. Minimize campfire impacts. Build fires only in designated areas.

6. Respect wildlife. Pack up your food and keep a safe distance from wildlife at all times.

7. Be considerate of other visitors. Avoid unnecessary noise, uncontrolled pets, and damaging any surroundings.

-- TIPS FOR COOKING OUTDOORS --

No camping trip is complete without the meals that nourish the adventure. These simple tips help make cooking outside enjoyable, delicious, and safe.

PLAN AND PREP FROM HOME

Any prep you can do from home saves a lot of stress at the campsite. Not only is there less work to do, but you also know that you have everything you need.

FREEZE MEALS AHEAD OF TIME

Unless meat items are frozen before leaving, they should only be kept out of the refrigerator for two hours at most. One of the best ways to keep food cold for a longer amount of time while camping is to freeze it before leaving. This is especially helpful for multi-day trips. Pack meals in resealable plastic bags and label them. As a bonus, frozen foods double as ice packs and help keep all the contents of your cooler cold and fresh for longer.

TEST YOUR STOVE BEFORE YOU GO

There's nothing worse than getting ready to cook and realizing your camp stove doesn't work or it's out of fuel. Make sure your stove is ready to use before you leave.

KEEP A GOOD SUPPLY OF HEAVY-DUTY TINFOIL

Tinfoil is handy for keeping food warm, cooking over the fire, and wrapping up leftovers. It is a must-have camping kitchen staple.

KEEP A CLEAN KITCHEN

In an effort to keep away small (and large) animals that might be interested in your food, it's imperative to keep a clean outdoor kitchen. This protects yourself, future campers, *and* the wildlife. Keep food locked up in your vehicle, a bear box, or hanging in a tree at least 12 feet high.

START YOUR CAMPFIRE WELL BEFORE YOU WANT TO COOK ON IT

Campfire coals can take a long time to get just right. Build a fire and let the flames burn down until the coals are just hot. Some parts will be glowing and others not—that is okay! It could take 30 to 45 minutes to have great coals so be patient, and be sure to start the fire at least 30 minutes before you want to cook on it.

USE SQUEEZE BOTTLES FOR EVERYTHING

Squeeze bottles save you from using extra utensils and make cooking (and cleanup) much easier. Use them for things like pancake batter, eggs, dressings, jelly, peanut butter, and condiments.

HEAT YOUR CLEANING WATER WHILE YOU EAT YOUR MEAL

Before you start eating, get water going in a pot on the campfire or stove so it's ready to use when you're done eating and want to start washing dishes.

BACKYARD CAMPING

There are times when traveling to a campsite is impossible due to weather, scheduling conflicts, or other factors out of your control. This is a great time to set up camp in your backyard! Not only is backyard camping fun, but it's also a good opportunity to practice sleeping in a tent and campsite cooking while still being close to at-home conveniences.

Many of the recipes in this book can easily be adapted for backyard camping. I recommend choosing a few of your favorites and trying them out at home before bringing them on the trail. This will also allow you to work out any family preferences before you head to a campsite.

TIPS FOR BACKYARD CAMPING:

→ Don't forget to bring some of the comforts of home while you practice sleeping outside. Stuffed animals, blankets, and lights help kids make the transition a little easier.

→ While you can bring some extras with you when camping close to home, avoid bringing the unnecessary items. In particular, leave the electronics behind! Camping is a chance to spend uninterrupted, quality time with loved ones.

→ Do the setup together. Part of the fun of camping is the teamwork required. Divide the camp jobs and be sure to assign jobs to the kids, too.

→ Play games, go on a little "hike" near your home, and make it fun!

→ Don't skip making a fire (if it is allowed, of course) and cook outside, especially if you have access to a grill.

PART I

CAR CAMPING

Car camping allows for a little more wiggle room than backcountry camping since you usually have the ability to bring more food and cooking supplies and can be more elaborate with your meals. Having easy access to those conveniences make it the preferred method of camping for most families.

This chapter will start with the basics of car camping to help make sure you have the essentials covered. Then I'll share with you my favorite car camping recipes organized by meal type.

That said, just because a recipe is listed in a certain section (breakfast, for example) doesn't mean it can't be enjoyed at another time, too. Of course, no camping trip is complete without some snacks and treats, so I've also included those.

CAR CAMPING ESSENTIALS

Car camping requires some basic essentials to help you find your own personal groove in your camp kitchen. What works well for one person or family may not be the best for another due to cooking equipment, conditions, or dietary needs.

I've outlined my best tips in this chapter to help you get set up and organized so that your meals can not only be delicious, but also efficient.

As I mentioned earlier, I hope you will be inspired to try a recipe that's a little out of your comfort zone or cook using a method you've never tried before. The recipes in this book are simple for anyone to execute, so you should feel free to experiment!

--- OUTDOOR KITCHEN CHECKLIST ---

Setting up your car camping kitchen starts with basic tools. These two lists are broken out into must-have items and ones that are optional, but nice to have (if you have room!).

MUST-HAVE ITEMS:

☐ Camping stove and fuel
☐ Can opener
☐ Cooking pot and lid
☐ Cooking spray
☐ Cooler
☐ Cutting board
☐ Frying pan
☐ Heavy-duty tinfoil
☐ Kitchen knife for cutting and chopping

☐ Large spoon
☐ Matches and/or lighter
☐ Paper towels
☐ Resealable plastic freezer bags
☐ Spatula
☐ Tongs
☐ Trash bags
☐ Whisk

NICE-TO-HAVE ITEMS:

☐ Camp table
☐ Cheese grater
☐ Containers for leftovers
☐ Firewood
☐ Hand-crank blender
☐ Lantern or headlamp

☐ Measuring cups and spoons
☐ Parchment paper and parchment paper liners for the Dutch oven
☐ Portable coffee/tea maker
☐ Roasting forks
☐ Rolling ice-cream maker

--- PANTRY STAPLES ---

Having basic pantry staples on hand and organized makes car camping easy.
Although these aren't absolutely necessary, especially if you're doing most of
the prep work at home, they are great to have around. When you're out camping,
plans sometimes change, and having staple items can make all the difference.

- ☐ Baking soda (for putting out grease fires)
- ☐ Boxed mac and cheese
- ☐ Canned beans
- ☐ Canned tuna
- ☐ Condiments (ketchup, mustard, hot sauce , etc.)
- ☐ Favorite seasonings
- ☐ Ground cinnamon
- ☐ Honey and/or maple syrup
- ☐ Noodles
- ☐ Oats
- ☐ Olive or coconut oil
- ☐ Rice
- ☐ Salt and black pepper

--- ORGANIZING YOUR --- OUTDOOR KITCHEN

Car camping allows you to bring a more complete kitchen setup than backpacking,
but it's still best to have the necessities organized for easy access.

→ Walk through each of the meals you will be cooking daily and what pots,
pans, and utensils you will need, and bring only those items.

→ Store foods in resealable plastic bags and label *everything* (ex: "breakfast day 1," "snacks day 2," etc.)

→ Have a dedicated plastic storage container with a lid for your outdoor kitchen (the container with the lid on can double as a table surface to wash dishes on) and make sure it can contain:

  → Any pots and pans you need

  → Utensils, which are more easily stored in a mesh bag or utensil organizer

  → Two tubs or collapsible sinks for washing and rinsing dishes

  → Biodegradable soap (found at most outdoor retailers or online) and a sponge

  → Hyper-absorbent towel(s) for drying dishes

→ Pack your cooler with pre-planned and frozen meals in reverse order so the ones you want first are at the top. Store condiments in this cooler also.

→ Use a second plastic lidded tote for dry foods.

HOW TO PACK A COOLER

Packing a cooler correctly goes a long way to help keep foods cold and fresh. I recommend starting with a high-quality cooler (they've come a long way in the last 20 years!), especially if you will be camping for multiple days in a row. If you're camping in bear country, also consider a bearproof cooler to maximize safety.

Before you pack your cooler, there are a few prep steps you can take to make the whole experience smoother and more efficient.

1. **Prep your food to save space:** This not only cuts down on unnecessary items in the cooler, but it also helps streamline your camp cooking. I also recommend getting rid of any extra packaging that is just taking up room.
2. **Go leakproof:** The likelihood of items getting wet in your cooler is very high. Consider this issue as you pack foods. Avoid containers that will leak or get soggy in wet conditions.
3. **Freeze everything you can:** Freezing meat and other foods that are easily frozen will help keep them and the foods around them cold longer.
4. **Refrigerate everything else:** Don't put anything in your cooler that is at room temperature. By getting every item cold in some capacity, you'll cut down on the energy needed to cool your cooler contents.
5. **Pre-freeze water bottles:** Frozen water bottles are a great way to build your cooler base with ice that won't make a mess when it melts. Just be sure to keep them three-quarters full to allow room for expansion.

→

6. **Pre-chill your cooler:** The night before you leave, fill your cooler with cold items so the cooler itself is starting cold before you even pack it. These items can be taken out in the morning, so it's totally okay to throw in any random frozen items. The less air in the cooler, the colder it will get.

The cooler should be the last item you throw in your car, so you'll want to be organized as you pack it. I recommend having a plan so you're not throwing everything in as you rush to get out the door.

1. Start with a layer of block ice on the bottom. You can use ice cubes or reusable ice packs if you need to, but I recommend starting with the afore-mentioned pre-frozen water bottles. Pack your food in reverse order from the last day's food on the bottom to the first day's food at the top. Remember to pack foods with liquids in them (even if they're frozen liquids) right-side up to avoid potential messes with melting.

2. Fill in the gaps with small food items and ice cubes. Large pockets of air will accelerate ice melt, so avoid them as much as you can.

→ Pack breakfast foods on the left, lunch foods in the middle, and dinner foods on the right so they're easy to find. You want your cooler lid closed as much as possible to keep the temperature stable, so it's best to avoid having to dig to find items. Packing a giant cooler? Consider mapping it out!

3 PLACE EGGS, SNACKS, DRINKS, PRODUCE, AND CONDIMENTS ON TOP. PUT PRODUCE IN BASKETS TO PROTECT FROM BEING CRUSHED.

2 PACK PREMADE MEALS IN REVERSE ORDER FROM THE LAST DAY'S FOOD ON THE BOTTOM TO THE FIRST DAY'S FOOD ON TOP.

1 PLACE BLOCK ICE, ICE CUBES, ICE PACKS, OR PRE-FROZEN WATER BOTTLES HERE.

--- METHODS FOR COOKING OUTDOORS ---

There are many different methods for cooking outdoors. The perfect choice for you is a combination of personal preference and the weather conditions at your campsite. A campfire is the classic go-to, but during high fire danger or heavy rain that won't be possible. Having a backup option is always a good idea.

-- USING A CAMP STOVE --

Avid car campers almost always keep a camp stove handy for cooking. Camp stoves can be lit and used in most weather conditions and are more dependable than a campfire. However, any recipe that can be made on a camp stove can also be adapted to be cooked over a campfire.

-- USING A GRATE --

In most established campgrounds, campfire rings include a grilling grate that you can flip over to use as a stable cooking surface. This can be used for directly cooking food (like kebabs or burgers) or for placing a pot or Dutch oven on it. You can also bring your own grate, which is my personal preference when I plan to cook food directly on it.

HOW TO BUILD A CAMPFIRE

Building a campfire is a pivotal camping skill that you should practice before you leave on a trip.

1. Find a safe location to build your fire. Always check local regulations in the area you are camping before building a fire.

2. If an established campfire ring is available, always use that. Confirm that nothing flammable is within 10 feet of the fire area, the area is sheltered from wind, and it's on level ground.

3. Gather dry wood and tinder of varying sizes. You will need small sticks, bark, wood shavings, or dry leaves for tinder. Dryer lint from home also works great as tinder. Kindling should be small sticks and branches. Fuel for the fire should be varying larger sizes of wood that will still fit in your campfire ring (so leave that huge dead tree where it is!). Remember, wood should not be gathered from green and live sources. Having a fire starter, even if only as a backup, is a great idea.

4. Lay your fire. I prefer the "tepee method" which starts with tinder in the center of your fire ring and then kindling and small fuel pieces building up around it in a tepee shape.

5. Light your fire! Start your tinder low and in the center to avoid it being blown out by the wind. Add fuel slowly and let it catch fire before adding more fuel.

6. After you're all done, the *most* important part of the whole process is making sure the fire is "dead out" and cold to the touch before you leave.

-- USING TINFOIL --

Tinfoil may possibly be the most versatile cooking tool in your outdoor kitchen. It helps with cleanup in Dutch ovens, packing up leftovers, and, our favorite, foil pack meals. You'll notice many of the recipes in this section are made in the folds of tinfoil.

-- USING CAST IRON --

I am a fan of cast iron, camping or not, but love that I can take it into the woods and not worry about it being banged around or burned. Cast iron is heavy and literally indestructible. We have three different cast-iron tools we use on a regular basis while camping:

SKILLET

This can be used on a camp stove or directly on the campfire.

DUTCH OVEN

Again, this can be used on a camp stove or directly in the coals of a campfire. It is your "oven away from home" and, with a little practice, can be used to cook almost any dish. Dutch oven cooking does take some patience to get coals just right and then careful observation, but the results make it worth learning.

PIE IRON SANDWICH MAKER

My kids' favorite cast-iron tool, this is a very fun way to make hot sandwiches over the campfire or, better yet, some of our favorite desserts.

CHAPTER 2

BREAKFAST

Start your day outdoors with a breakfast that will keep your belly full and energy high. This chapter includes a variety of meals that will suit an array of dietary needs and taste preferences. Some recipes are light and fast, and others are meant to be cooked as you enjoy your coffee or tea around a morning campfire.

HOMEMADE INSTANT OATMEAL

DAIRY-FREE, VEGAN

SERVES 6 / **PREP TIME:** 10 MINUTES / **COOK TIME:** 5 MINUTES

My kids love having their own individual oatmeal packets, but I can't stand the amount of sugar that's typically in store-bought oatmeal. This recipe is a great alternative that allows you to not only know what is actually going into breakfast, but also has room for customization.

3 cups old-fashioned oats

¾ cup dried fruit (Craisins, raisins, apricots, apples, blueberries, etc.)

¾ cup nuts

¼ cup brown sugar

2 tablespoons cinnamon

2 tablespoons flaxseed meal

1 teaspoon nutmeg

½ teaspoon ground cloves

3½ cups water, divided

PREP AT HOME

1. In a large bowl, combine all the ingredients and mix well. If you're packing the oatmeal for different tastes, leave the fruit out until it is already portioned and let everyone add fruit to taste to their baggies.

2. Portion the mixture into six snack-size resealable plastic bags for easy packing.

AT THE CAMPSITE

3. Boil 3 cups of water on a stove or on the fire.

4. Pour the contents of your oatmeal baggie into a heat-resistant bowl.

5. Add about ½ cup of water to the bowl and let sit for 5 minutes before serving.

BISCUITS AND GRAVY

NUT-FREE

SERVES 4 TO 6 / **PREP TIME:** 25 MINUTES / **COOK TIME:** 15 MINUTES

Biscuits and gravy was a breakfast I always passed on as a kid, but my own children have claimed it as worthy of all birthdays and special occasions. To simplify the process at the campsite, the biscuits are made at home and the gravy is made fresh at the site.

FOR THE BISCUITS

2½ cups all-purpose flour

2 tablespoons baking powder

1 teaspoon salt

½ cup unsalted butter, cold and cubed

1 cup cold buttermilk

FOR THE GRAVY

1 (12-ounce) package maple-flavored sausage

3 tablespoons butter

⅓ cup all-purpose flour

3 cups milk

Salt and black pepper

TO PREP THE BISCUITS AT HOME

1. Preheat the oven to 425°F. Line a baking sheet with parchment paper.
2. In a large bowl, whisk together the flour, baking powder, and salt until combined.
3. Incorporate the cubed butter into the dry ingredients with a pastry cutter until coarse crumbs form.
4. Add the buttermilk and stir until just combined. Do not overwork the dough as this makes the biscuits less flaky. The dough will be dry.
5. Turn the dough onto a lightly floured surface and flatten into a large rectangle. Fold the short side over and press the dough until it's about ¾ inch thick.

CONTINUED>

6. Use a 3-inch round cookie cutter to cut the dough into circles and arrange so the biscuits are barely touching on the baking sheet.
7. Bake for 13 to 15 minutes until the tops are just slightly golden brown.
8. Let cool and store in an airtight container or resealable plastic bag in the refrigerator until ready to take camping.

TO MAKE THE GRAVY AT THE CAMPSITE

9. Brown the sausage in a large skillet over the fire or on a camp stove over medium-high heat. Once browned, add the butter and stir until melted.
10. Add the flour and mix to cover the sausage and cook for a minute.
11. Add the milk and stir continuously, scraping the bottom, until the gravy thickens, about 10 minutes.
12. Add salt and pepper to taste. Serve the gravy warm over the biscuits.

TIP: We don't always have buttermilk around, so we are often doing some substitutions. Whole milk works fine, or you can use powdered buttermilk, which you can find in the baking aisle.

VEGETARIAN BREAKFAST BURRITOS

NUT-FREE, VEGETARIAN

SERVES 6 / PREP TIME: 35 MINUTES / COOK TIME: 10 MINUTES

Of all the breakfasts I make, at home or on the trail, these burritos are my favorite. They are perfect for busy days at the campsite when everyone needs a hot breakfast to give them lots of energy, and also great for customizing depending on ingredients on hand or personal preferences. The burritos are packed with ingredients to keep you going all day long.

2 sweet potatoes

3 tablespoons olive or grapeseed oil, divided

Salt and black pepper

6 large eggs, whisked

1 (15-ounce) can black beans

6 burrito-size whole-wheat tortillas

2 cups shredded Cheddar cheese

Salsa, for topping (optional)

Avocado, for topping (optional)

PREP AT HOME

1. Preheat the oven to 400°F and line a large baking sheet with tinfoil.

2. Chop the sweet potatoes into ¼-inch pieces and toss in a large bowl or resealable plastic bag with 2 tablespoons of oil and the salt and pepper to taste.

3. Arrange the potatoes on the baking sheet in an even layer.

4. Cook for 20 minutes, turning once or until the potatoes are lightly browned and easy to puncture with a fork.

CONTINUED>

5. In a large skillet, heat the remaining 1 tablespoon of oil over medium heat. Add the eggs and scramble until cooked through, then mix in the black beans.

6. On each tortilla, lay ⅓ cup of Cheddar cheese, then layer the egg and bean mixture, sweet potatoes, and a spoonful of salsa and sliced avocado (if using).

7. Wrap each burrito in heavy-duty tinfoil (sometimes I like to add an extra layer of foil for good measure!), then refrigerate until ready to transfer to a cooler for transporting to the campsite.

AT THE CAMPSITE

8. Warm your burritos on fire coals directly in the tinfoil or, if you can't have a fire, in a pan on your camp stove.

TIP: Add a pound of breakfast sausage (sage or maple flavor are my favorites) for extra protein.

BLUEBERRY BREAKFAST BAKE

NUT-FREE, VEGETARIAN

SERVES 6 / **PREP TIME:** 10 MINUTES / **COOK TIME:** 45 MINUTES

This recipe isn't healthy by any means, but it's delicious and a great dish for celebrating birthdays (or any occasion) on the trail. After baking, the dish has the consistency of bread pudding and is delicious just torn apart as you eat. We eat it family-style, gathered around the dish, with our hands.

6 large eggs

½ cup milk

½ cup heavy (whipping) cream

1 teaspoon vanilla extract

2 cups fresh blueberries, divided

1 loaf cinnamon bread, sliced

Maple syrup, for serving

Whipped cream for serving (optional)

PREP AT HOME

1. Whisk together the eggs, milk, heavy cream, and vanilla in a container with a leakproof lid, then refrigerate until ready to use.

2. Wash the blueberries and put them in a lidded container for transportation.

AT THE CAMPSITE

3. Lay two large sheets of heavy-duty tinfoil on top of each other. Spray with nonstick cooking spray. Place the loaf of cinnamon bread in the middle and fold up the edges to make a bowl around the loaf. This will keep the raw egg mixture from escaping.

CONTINUED>

4. Spread the slices of bread apart and sprinkle 1 cup of blueberries over the loaf, making sure they get in between each slice of bread. Press them there if needed.

5. Pour the egg mixture over the loaf evenly, ensuring it goes in between each of the bread slices.

6. Use another large piece of foil to completely cover the loaf and crimp the edges of the top and bottom pieces of foil to seal.

7. Place the loaf on the campfire grate over hot coals. Grill until the egg is cooked through, about 30 minutes. Make sure to keep it away from any flames and rotate every 5 minutes to prevent burning.

8. Remove from heat and let cool in the foil for 10 minutes.

9. Serve slices topped with remaining blueberries, syrup, and whipped cream (if using).

FRUIT AND YOGURT PARFAIT CONES

VEGETARIAN

SERVES 4 / **PREP TIME:** 5 MINUTES / **ASSEMBLY TIME:** 5 MINUTES

My kids think they're getting dessert when we plan this special breakfast. It's a fun way to start the day with smiles and cut down on camp-side dishes. To reduce sugar, I use plain yogurt and let the sweetness come from the fruit. This is also a great recipe for kids to do on their own (though remind them to use gentle hands so they don't crush the cones).

Assorted fruit (strawberries, blueberries, bananas, raspberries, blackberries, mandarin oranges, grapes, etc.)

4 waffle cones

2 cups plain or vanilla yogurt

2 cups granola

PREP AT HOME

1. Wash and cut the fruit and store in leakproof containers for travel to your campsite (if using bananas, slice just before assembling the parfaits).

AT THE CAMPSITE

2. Carefully take a cone and add a spoonful of yogurt to the bottom. Then layer a spoonful of fruit and a spoonful of granola.

3. Continue layering the cones with yogurt, fruit, and granola until the cones are full, finishing with granola on top.

LUMBERJACK BREAKFAST

GLUTEN-FREE

SERVES 4 / **PREP TIME:** 10 MINUTES / **COOK TIME:** 20 MINUTES

Everyone loves to help prep these foil packet breakfasts that have loads of flavor and are made to order. This is another recipe that is very easy to customize—add in whatever veggies and breakfast meat you love. It can be made over the hot coals of a campfire or on a grill. Add your favorite seasonings—hot sauce, steak seasoning, salt and pepper, or Cajun sauce are all great options.

1 (16-link) package breakfast sausages

1 (15-ounce) bag frozen hash browns

1 cup chopped green bell peppers

1 cup chopped onions

8 eggs

1 (8-ounce) package shredded Cheddar cheese

Salt and black pepper

Salsa, for topping (optional)

Guacamole, for topping (optional)

1. Prepare 4 large squares of tinfoil and lightly spray them with cooking spray. Fold the edges up slightly to form a bit of a bowl shape so the eggs are contained when you add them.

2. Place 4 sausages in each piece of foil.

3. Add a handful of the hash browns (leftover potatoes work well, too), ¼ cup of bell peppers, ¼ cup of onions, and 2 eggs. Add salt and black pepper to taste.

4. Wrap up the packet, making sure each side is closed securely. Double wrap with tinfoil.

5. Cook over fire or on the grill for 15 to 20 minutes, turning each packet once.

6. After 15 minutes, open the packet to check that the sausage is cooked through. Add about 2 ounces of Cheddar cheese to each packet, close them up, and cook for 5 more minutes to melt the cheese.
7. Remove from heat and let cool slightly.
8. Top with salsa and guacamole (if using), and eat right out of the foil.

TIP: Wake up early to get the fire going for this breakfast. The packets cook best over coals that are hot but without flame.

WHOLE-WHEAT BANANA BREAD PANCAKES

NUT-FREE, VEGETARIAN

SERVES 4 / PREP TIME: 5 MINUTES / COOK TIME: 15 MINUTES

My family loves these pancakes so much, especially for camping. They are filling and just sweet enough. They also taste great cold—perfect for a snack on the trail later.

1 cup whole-wheat pastry flour

2 teaspoons baking powder

2 teaspoons cinnamon

⅛ teaspoon nutmeg

¼ teaspoon salt

1 egg

1 teaspoon vanilla

½ cup milk

2 ripe bananas, mashed

1 tablespoon butter, plus more for topping

Chocolate chips, for topping (optional)

Whipped cream, for topping (optional)

Syrup, for topping (optional)

PREP AT HOME

1. In a large resealable plastic bag, mix together the flour, baking powder, cinnamon, nutmeg, and salt.

2. In a separate leakproof container (I recommend a water bottle), combine the egg, vanilla, and milk and refrigerate, then transfer to a cooler for transporting to the campsite.

AT THE CAMPSITE

3. Carefully mash the bananas directly in their peels. Add the bananas to the bag of dry ingredients and peel and mash further with your hands or a fork to incorporate well.

4. Add the egg, vanilla, and milk to the bag with the dry ingredients. Seal and mix well by shaking and massaging. The batter will be thick.

5. Lightly coat a large skillet or griddle with 1 tablespoon of butter. Place on the fire grate.

6. Drop about ¼ cup of batter onto the skillet and spread it out slightly with the scoop. Repeat with the remaining batter until the skillet is full (try to keep the pancakes from touching).

7. Add a few chocolate chips (if using).

8. Cook until bubbles appear on top, about 2 minutes.

9. Flip pancakes and cook until golden brown, another 2 minutes.

10. Serve with whipped cream, syrup, and butter (if using).

TIP: Though leakproof storage containers have their place, I find that transporting eggs and other wet ingredients works best in a water bottle like a Nalgene. Not only can you rest easy knowing the leakproof lid is doing its job, but it also makes it easier to pour the batter when cooking.

CAMPFIRE FRENCH TOAST

NUT-FREE, VEGETARIAN

SERVES 4 TO 6 / PREP TIME: 10 MINUTES / COOK TIME: 1½ HOURS

Since it's made in a Dutch oven, this dish becomes more of a French toast casserole. Though it does take some time to cook when you factor in the 20-minute soak time, that provides an opportunity for you to plan your day's activities while the Dutch oven does all the work. To cut down on the time it takes to make this dish, you can do most of the prep work at home so it's easy to make the fire, dump the ingredients in, and cook while others are waking up.

4 tablespoons sugar

1 teaspoon cinnamon

¼ teaspoon nutmeg

¼ teaspoon ground cloves

¼ teaspoon salt

4 eggs

1½ cups plus 2 tablespoons milk, divided

¾ cup powdered sugar

2 teaspoons vanilla extract

1 (16-ounce) loaf French bread

PREP AT HOME

1. Mix the sugar, cinnamon, nutmeg, cloves, salt, eggs, and 1½ cups of milk in a container with a leakproof lid and refrigerate until ready to use.

2. Add the powdered sugar, the remaining 2 tablespoons of milk, and the vanilla to a small resealable plastic bag, mix well and refrigerate until ready to use. (This mixture is the powdered sugar glaze.)

3. Cut the French bread into ¾-inch chunks and put in a large resealable plastic bag.

AT THE CAMPSITE

4. Line the Dutch oven with a layer of tinfoil or parchment paper to make cleanup easy. Alternatively, spray the bottom and sides of the Dutch oven down well with cooking spray.

5. Place the bread in the bottom of the Dutch oven. Cover evenly with the egg mixture.

6. Let stand 20 to 30 minutes to allow the bread to soak up all the liquid.

7. While you wait, build a fire and let it burn down to the coals.

8. To cook this at about 350°F, you will need to place 9 charcoal briquettes on the bottom and 15 on top of the lid. Since it needs to cook for 40 to 50 minutes, it's best to keep some fire going on another part of the fire ring so you can replenish cold briquettes partway through.

9. Every 15 minutes, turn the Dutch oven bottom a quarter turn in one direction and the Dutch oven lid a quarter turn in the opposite direction to ensure even cooking.

10. Cook for 40 to 50 minutes or until the egg mixture is cooked through.

11. Drizzle with the powdered sugar glaze and serve warm.

TIP: Check every 10 to 15 minutes to prevent burning. If the edges are browning too quickly, remove some of the bottom coals to prevent burning while the middle is cooking.

BACON AND EGG CHEESY GRITS

GLUTEN-FREE, NUT-FREE

SERVES 4 / **PREP TIME:** 5 MINUTES / **COOK TIME:** 10 MINUTES

Grits make for a fabulous and filling breakfast option, especially with lots of cheese and bacon, which provides both protein and flavor. My kids were initially hesitant to try grits at all, but it didn't take long for them to declare this a favorite breakfast.

8 strips bacon, cooked and crumbled

1 cup shredded Cheddar cheese

1 cup quick gluten-free grits

Salt and black pepper

4 eggs

PREP AT HOME

1. Cook the bacon, then cool and crumble it.
2. Pack the Cheddar cheese in a container or small resealable plastic bag and pack the bacon in a separate resealable plastic bag.
3. Store both bags in the refrigerator, then transfer to a cooler for transporting to the campsite.

AT THE CAMPSITE

4. In a large pot, cook the grits according to the package directions (it should take about 5 minutes).
5. Meanwhile, fry the eggs in a skillet as desired so they are ready when the grits are.

6. As soon as the grits thicken, remove from heat and mix in the shredded cheese and salt and pepper to taste.
7. Divide the grits among four bowls or plates and add a fried egg on top of each.
8. Divide the crumbled bacon evenly among the bowls and serve.

APPLE GINGER WALNUT MUFFINS

VEGETARIAN

MAKES 12 MUFFINS / **PREP TIME:** 15 MINUTES / **COOK TIME:** 15 MINUTES

My family never goes on a camping trip without these muffins. I make them before leaving for a trip, freeze them, and bring them along for a breakfast or snack on the go. Delicious at any time of day, these muffins are a perfect combination of sweet and spice.

1¾ cups white whole-wheat flour

1½ teaspoons baking powder

½ teaspoon baking soda

1½ teaspoons ground cinnamon

¼ teaspoon ground ginger

½ teaspoon salt

1½ cups apple, chopped in small pieces

⅓ cup melted butter

½ cup maple syrup

2 eggs

½ cup plain Greek yogurt

½ cup applesauce

1 cup walnuts, chopped

1 teaspoon vanilla

1. Preheat the oven to 425°F. Grease a muffin tin with cooking spray or line with paper liners.

2. In a large mixing bowl, combine the flour, baking powder, baking soda, cinnamon, ginger, and salt. Add in the chopped apple and mix well.

3. In a medium bowl, whisk together the butter and maple syrup. Add the eggs and whisk again. Then add the yogurt, applesauce, walnuts, and vanilla and mix well.

4. Pour the wet ingredients into the dry and mix until just combined.

5. Divide the batter evenly among 12 muffin cups.

6. Bake muffins for 13 to 16 minutes or until golden on top and a toothpick comes out clean.

7. Store in sealed hard plastic containers or (carefully) in resealable plastic bags.

BACON, EGG, AND AVOCADO SANDWICH

NUT-FREE

SERVES 4 / **COOK TIME: 20 MINUTES**

This recipe may be our favorite one-pan breakfast. For a large group, you can make up to four sandwiches at a time using a very large skillet. You will be frying these sandwiches right in the bacon grease, which makes them incredibly yummy.

8 slices bacon, cut in half

8 slices bread

4 eggs

2 avocados

Sprouts, for topping (optional)

4 tomato slices (optional)

2 cups spinach (optional)

Salt and black pepper

1. Set the cast-iron skillet over your campfire or camp stove.

2. Place bacon in the skillet and cook over medium-low heat until crispy to your preference. Remove and place on a paper towel–lined plate to drain the excess grease.

3. If there is more than a half inch or so of bacon grease left in the pan, drain it slightly into a glass or can and reserve.

4. Toast the bread in the skillet in the bacon grease, flipping after about a minute until both sides are golden brown. Remove and set aside.

5. Fry your eggs in the skillet, one at a time, using a bit of the reserved grease if needed.

6. To assemble the sandwich, slice the avocado in half, discard the pit, and mash half the avocado onto both sides of the bread. Layer with the bacon and egg, then top with the sprouts, tomatoes, and spinach (if using), and salt and pepper to taste. Add the top toast piece and enjoy!

TIP: I recommend experimenting with different kinds of hearty breads (sourdough, seed, wheat, or leftover French toast!). To cut down on cook time or avoid bacon smells in bear country, you can pre-cook the bacon at home and fry the bread in butter or oil.

BACON KEBABS

DAIRY-FREE, GLUTEN-FREE, NUT-FREE

SERVES 4 / **PREP TIME:** 5 MINUTES / **COOK TIME:** 20 TO 30 MINUTES

Although I wouldn't necessarily recommend making this recipe in high bear country, it is an absolute favorite and a great way to make crispy bacon while camping. Don't be fooled by the fact that it is a one-ingredient dish. Bacon cooked over a fire is nothing like bacon pan-fried, but it's worth the extra effort. You'll need skewers for this recipe—I prefer the metal variety.

1 (16-ounce) package
thick-cut bacon

1. Weave each strip of bacon onto a skewer, being sure not to weave too tightly. Aim to have 3 to 4 pieces of bacon on each skewer.

2. Prepare a campfire with two logs or rocks on each side of the fire so you can rest the skewers between them.

3. Rotate the skewers every 5 minutes until done, about 30 minutes.

> **TIP:** When a campfire isn't possible, I often make kebabs at home right on the grill. Keep the heat low and watch carefully for grease fires, and be prepared with heat-safe gloves or hot pads to remove the skewers when ready.

CHAPTER 3

LUNCH AND DINNER

When camping, it's so easy to get stuck in a bit of a meal rut. The key is keeping things quick and easy, but that doesn't mean you have to eat the same things over and over. I certainly tend to reserve some meals *just* for camping, but I appreciate having a variety of options. Lunches tend to be quick and easy, whereas dinners celebrate family time around the fire. You'll find some of my family's favorite meals to eat around the campfire in this chapter.

CONTINUED>

CONTINUED

CAMPFIRE HASH

DAIRY-FREE, GLUTEN-FREE

SERVES 6 / COOK TIME: 35 MINUTES

There's just something about meat and potatoes after a long day outdoors that really hits the spot. This hash has a unique flavor from the chiles and uses corn, which is a nice break from the traditional potatoes and bacon.

2 tablespoons olive oil

1 large onion, chopped

2 garlic cloves, minced

1 (16-ounce) bag frozen cubed hash browns

1 pound smoked kielbasa or another sausage of your choice

1 (15-ounce) can whole kernel corn, drained

1 (4-ounce) can chopped green chiles

Salt and black pepper

Ketchup or hot sauce, for topping (optional)

1. Heat the olive oil in a large skillet over medium heat. Add the onion and cook until tender. Add the garlic and stir to combine.

2. Add the hash browns. Cook, uncovered, for about 20 minutes, stirring occasionally until tender.

3. Add the kielbasa, stir, and cook for another 10 minutes until browned.

4. Add the corn and chiles. Stir and cook for another 5 minutes or until heated through. Add salt and pepper to taste.

5. Serve with ketchup or hot sauce (if using).

TIP: If you prefer, you can certainly peel and cube fresh potatoes instead of using frozen ones. Count on using 4 large potatoes or 6 smaller ones. This recipe is forgiving and easy to adjust as necessary.

CHICKEN FAJITA FOIL PACKETS

DAIRY-FREE, GLUTEN-FREE, NUT-FREE

SERVES 4 / PREP TIME: 20 MINUTES / COOK TIME: 30 MINUTES

Though I usually make these foil packets over a campfire, they are just as delicious made in an oven at home while backyard camping. Note that the packets will cook faster in an oven than over a campfire. To simplify the prep process, I like to prep them completely at home and leave them in the cooler until it's time to cook.

1½ cups minute rice

1½ cups water

2 tablespoons taco or fajita seasoning (1 packet), divided

1 pound skinless, boneless chicken breasts, cut into thin strips

1 large yellow onion, cut into thin strips

2 bell peppers (any color), cut into thin strips

1 bag 6-inch flour tortillas

Guacamole, for topping (optional)

PREP AT HOME

1. Place the minute rice in a baggie and add water and 1 tablespoon of taco seasoning (or half a packet). Let sit for 5 minutes to allow the rice to start to absorb the liquid.

2. In a large bowl, combine the chicken breast, onion, and bell pepper. Add the remaining tablespoon of taco seasoning (or rest of the packet). Mix well, making sure the chicken and veggies are evenly coated.

3. Lay out 4 large sheets of tinfoil and fold up the sides, pinching to create walls. Spray each generously with cooking spray.

4. Divide the rice (and any leftover liquid) evenly among each sheet of tinfoil.
5. Top the rice evenly with the chicken, onions, and peppers.
6. Fold the foil over top of the dinners and wrap the sides tightly.
7. If cooking over a fire, wrap each packet with a second layer of tinfoil.
8. Keep refrigerated until ready to cook, or keep in a cooler if you're traveling to your camping area.

AT THE CAMPSITE

9. Make a fire and let it burn down to hot coals. Place the foil packets on top of the coals.
10. Cook for about 30 minutes over hot coals, turning every 10 minutes. (I recommend opening a packet after 20 minutes to check for doneness.)
11. Let cool for 5 minutes. Open packets carefully and enjoy with tortillas and the guacamole (if using).

> **TIP:** In addition to guacamole, you can top off the fajita packets with salsa, sour cream, and/or lime.

CAMPFIRE PIZZA LOGS

NUT-FREE

SERVES 4 / PREP TIME: 15 MINUTES / COOK TIME: 30 MINUTES

This is a super easy recipe and is such a treat for my pizza-loving family. We usually end up making a few logs and mixing up the toppings on each one for variety. Feel free to experiment with your own toppings. This can obviously be made to suit vegetarian diets, as you choose what you put on your pizza. Don't worry if the premade dough you find is an ounce or two over or under the weight given; it will still turn out beautifully.

1 (13.8-ounce) can premade pizza dough

1 (8-ounce) can pizza sauce

1 tablespoon Italian seasoning

2 cups shredded mozzarella cheese

OPTIONAL TOPPINGS

Pepperoni

Canned pineapple tidbits

Mushrooms

Diced ham

PREP AT HOME

1. Roll out the pizza dough to form a large rectangle, about ¼ inch thick, though you can experiment a bit for your own preferences.

2. Spread the pizza sauce over the top evenly, covering the entire rectangle.

3. Top with Italian seasoning, mozzarella, and desired toppings.

4. Roll the pizza to form a log, starting on the long side. (If you roll from the short side it will take much longer to cook since it will be thicker.)

5. Wrap in heavy-duty foil, then wrap in foil again. Refrigerate for 2 to 3 days and keep in a cooler for transporting to your campsite. If you're freezing it, take it out of the freezer right before leaving and be sure to let it thaw before cooking (while still wrapped in foil).

AT THE CAMPSITE

6. While still in the foil, cook on a hot grill (if car camping), or on the grill of a firepit.

7. Cook for 15 minutes, flip, then cook about 15 minutes longer.

8. In the foil, slice the pizza into about 1-inch-thick rounds, and serve it up for all to enjoy!

> **TIP:** Not into canned pizza dough? This recipe works with homemade pizza dough, too. The trick is to get the dough thin and be prepared to move it so all sides cook evenly, especially if you're doing so over the fire.

LOADED BAKED SWEET POTATOES

GLUTEN-FREE, VEGETARIAN

SERVES 4 / **PREP TIME:** 5 MINUTES / **COOK TIME:** 30 MINUTES

This is a great recipe to make around the campfire on chilly camping nights, and perfect for when you don't have a stove or grill to cook on. You can definitely make this recipe with homemade chili, but canned chili just makes it easier and there are some fantastic options out there.

2 scallions

1½ cups Cheddar cheese (optional)

4 medium sweet potatoes

1 can vegetarian chili

1 avocado, cubed

Sour cream, for topping (optional)

PREP AT HOME

1. Slice your scallions and pack in a resealable plastic bag.
2. Shred the Cheddar cheese (if using) at home and pack in another resealable plastic bag.
3. Keep refrigerated until ready to use, or keep in a cooler if you're traveling to your camping area.

AT THE CAMPSITE

4. Wrap each of the sweet potatoes in heavy-duty foil and put them in the hot coals of your fire. Cook for about 30 minutes, turning them every 5 minutes using hot pads or tongs so they cook evenly.

5. While the potatoes are cooking, heat up the can of chili in a separate pot either over the fire or on your camping stove.

6. After about 30 minutes, once the potatoes are soft and cooked through, take them out of the fire. Let cool for about 5 minutes.

7. Carefully unwrap the foil, slice the potatoes down the middle, and top them with the chili and avocado.

8. Top with sour cream and Cheddar cheese (if using).

TIP: These potatoes can be eaten directly in the foil to cut down on dirty dishes. When cooking on the fire, I recommend checking them after 25 minutes for doneness.

PREMADE CAMP SANDWICHES

NUT-FREE

SERVES 4 TO 6 / **PREP TIME:** 15 MINUTES / **COOK TIME:** 15 MINUTES

Save yourself some time at the campsite and prep these sandwiches entirely from home. Then all you have to do is make a fire and throw them on once you get there. The buttery mustard sauce with the ham and cheese is a combination that makes these sandwiches irresistible around the fire. They are a bit messy, though, so be prepared with napkins when eating them.

12 Hawaiian rolls

1 pound sliced deli ham

12 slices Swiss cheese

1 (16-ounce) package bacon, cooked and cooled (optional)

½ cup butter, melted

1½ tablespoons Dijon mustard

1 tablespoon dried onion

1 tablespoon brown sugar

PREP AT HOME

1. Keeping the entire package of rolls together, slice them in half so you have a sheet of "tops" and a sheet of "bottoms."

2. Cut a large sheet of tinfoil and position the bottoms on it, cut-sides up.

3. Lay half the ham over the bottom sheet of rolls, then lay half the Swiss cheese over the ham.

4. Repeat with a layer of ham and a layer of cheese, so you have four layers on top of the rolls.

5. Add the bacon (if using).

6. Carefully lay the top sheet of rolls on top of the cheese.

7. Roll up the sides of tinfoil to form a "bowl."
8. In a small bowl, combine the butter, Dijon mustard, dried onion, and brown sugar. Pour the mixture evenly over the top of the sandwiches, making sure to keep the liquid inside the foil.
9. Add another layer of tinfoil on top and seal the edges.
10. Keep refrigerated until ready to cook, or store in a cooler if you're traveling to your camping area.

AT THE CAMPSITE
11. Place the package of sandwiches on a grill over the fire.
12. Cook, turning frequently, until the cheese is melted and lightly toasted, about 10 minutes.
13. Remove from fire and let cool slightly. Unwrap the foil and cut along the roll lines to make 12 individual sandwiches.

TIP: This recipe also works great on a grill. If you prefer, you can also make individual sandwiches and wrap each one separately.

LOADED MAC AND CHEESE

NUT-FREE, VEGETARIAN

SERVES 4 TO 6 / **PREP TIME:** 15 MINUTES / **COOK TIME:** 20 MINUTES

Mac and cheese is such a satisfying comfort food, which makes it perfect for camping. In an effort to get my kids to eat more veggies, I like to load mine up with them to make this mac and cheese a balanced meal in one pot. This recipe is made even easier by doing all of the prep work at home. You'll need a large rectangular aluminum foil pan for this one.

1 (7-ounce) package elbow macaroni noodles

½ cup heavy cream

3 tablespoons butter

1 cup grated sharp Cheddar cheese

1 cup grated Parmesan cheese

½ cup Gouda cheese

Salt and black pepper

Dash paprika

1½ cups frozen mixed veggies

2 cups potato chips, crushed

PREP AT HOME

1. Cook your noodles according to the package directions and drain.
2. Stir the heavy cream into the cooked pasta, then add the butter and cheeses and mix well.
3. Sprinkle with the paprika and add salt and pepper to taste.
4. Add the mixed veggies and stir well.
5. Line a 9-by-13-inch pan with foil, then spray with nonstick cooking spray.
6. Pour the pasta into the prepared pan.

7. Top with the crushed potato chips.
8. Spray one side of a piece of foil with cooking spray, then cover the pan, greased-side down.
9. Refrigerate until ready to cook, or keep in a cooler if you're traveling to your camping area.

AT THE CAMPSITE

10. Place the pan on the fire grate above hot coals.
11. Cook for about 20 minutes until hot and bubbly, making sure not to burn the bottom.

> **TIP:** If you want to double the recipe, I suggest doing each batch in its own pan so it cooks evenly. Use butter crackers instead of potato chips to add a different flavor and texture to the mac and cheese topping.

DUTCH OVEN VEGETARIAN LASAGNA

NUT-FREE, VEGETARIAN

SERVES 6 / PREP TIME: 15 MINUTES / COOK TIME: 30 MINUTES

Lasagna is a family favorite and a filling, comforting meal for camping. This recipe makes a lot, so I love to share with friends or plan on saving leftovers for the next day.

8 ounces fresh mushrooms, sliced

2 cups baby spinach

1 box lasagna noodles

1 tablespoon olive oil

3 cups shredded mozzarella cheese, divided

1 cup ricotta cheese

1 cup cottage cheese

½ cup shredded Parmesan cheese

2 eggs

1 (24-ounce) jar spaghetti sauce

PREP AT HOME

1. Wash and slice your mushrooms. Wash your spinach if necessary.

2. Pack your spinach and mushrooms together in a resealable plastic bag.

3. Cook the lasagna noodles according to the package. Once cool, add the olive oil to prevent sticking and pack in a resealable plastic bag.

4. Combine 2 cups of mozzarella cheese, the ricotta cheese, cottage cheese, Parmesan cheese, and eggs and mix well. Put this mixture in a resealable plastic bag.

5. Refrigerate the cheese mixture, vegetables, and noodles until ready to cook, or keep in a cooler if you're traveling to your camping area.

AT THE CAMPSITE

6. Line your Dutch oven with parchment paper or tinfoil.
7. Place a single layer of noodles on the bottom.
8. Add a layer of spaghetti sauce (about ¾ cup).
9. Add about one-third of the cheese mixture and spread evenly over the sauce.
10. Add about half of the mushroom and spinach mixture.
11. Repeat the layers (noodles, sauce, cheese mixture, mushrooms and spinach).
12. End with one more layer of sauce and then sprinkle the remaining 1 cup of mozzarella cheese on top.
13. Put the lid on the Dutch oven.
14. Place the Dutch oven on coals equivalent to 12 briquettes. Add coals equivalent to 12 briquettes on top.
15. Cook for about 20 minutes until hot and bubbly.
16. Scoop the lasagna directly out of the pot and serve.

TIP: You can easily add a pound of ground sausage to this, if desired. If you don't have fresh spinach, use 1½ cups of frozen chopped spinach.

WALKING TACOS

GLUTEN-FREE, NUT-FREE

SERVES 4 TO 6 / PREP TIME: 15 MINUTES / COOK TIME: 10 MINUTES

This is THE favorite recipe of my kids—mostly because I let them eat chips out of their own bag. Corn chips aren't exactly healthy, but they're great in these tacos. And the salty crunch is perfect after a long, tiring day outside.

1 pound ground beef

1 tablespoon chili powder

1 teaspoon ground cumin

¾ teaspoon salt

½ teaspoon dried oregano

½ teaspoon garlic powder

¼ teaspoon black pepper

⅓ cup chopped onion

½ cup tomato sauce

¼ cup water

½ cup Cheddar cheese

1 medium tomato, chopped

½ cup lettuce

4 (1-ounce) bags corn chips

Guacamole (optional)

PREP AT HOME

1. Brown the beef. Add the chili powder, cumin, salt, oregano, garlic powder, and pepper and stir well.

2. Add the onions and stir well.

3. Reduce the heat to medium and add the tomato sauce and the water. Stir to combine. Cook for 7 to 8 minutes until slightly thickened.

4. Let the beef cool, then pack it in a large resealable plastic bag or sealable container to transport to the campsite.

5. Shred the Cheddar cheese, chop the tomatoes, and shred the lettuce. Divide the toppings evenly into 4 to 6 individual resealable plastic bags.

6. Keep everything refrigerated until ready to cook, or keep in a cooler if you're traveling to your camping area.

7. Warm the beef and onion mixture over a fire or camp stove in a medium-size pan.

8. Crush the corn chips slightly before you cut open the bags.

9. Add the beef and toppings right to the chip bag and eat!

> **TIP:** If your crowd has larger appetites and the chip bags aren't big enough, you can easily make these tacos in bowls and top them with the corn chips. This recipe also tastes great with tortilla chips.

GRILLED PIZZA SANDWICHES

NUT-FREE, VEGETARIAN OPTION

SERVES 6 / **PREP TIME:** 10 MINUTES / **COOK TIME:** 10 MINUTES

These pizza sandwiches are a great alternative to my Campfire Pizza Logs (page 42) if your family likes to customize their meals. Since they are smaller in size, they cook faster, too, feeding your crowd of hungry campers quickly. I've listed some topping ideas below, but these are just ideas. I do recommend arriving at camp with all your toppings prepped and ready to put right on the pizzas.

1 (6-count) package English muffins

1 (15-ounce) can pizza sauce

2 cups shredded mozzarella cheese

1 (6-ounce) package sliced pepperoni (optional)

Sausage, cooked, for topping (optional)

Mixed chopped vegetables, for topping (optional)

1. Open up the English muffins. Cover each side (12 total) with pizza sauce.
2. Sprinkle cheese on top of the pizza sauce on 6 of the slices.
3. Add the sliced pepperoni and sausage (if using), and any desired veggies on top of the cheese.
4. Add another layer of cheese on each slice.
5. Top each sandwich with one of the sauce-covered muffin slices.

6. Put the sandwich in a pie iron, or alternatively, wrap in foil.
7. Grill the sandwiches over the fire for about 5 minutes per side. If in foil, place them on a campfire grate.
8. Let cool slightly before unwrapping.

TIP: Let your crowd choose their toppings! You can use pineapple pieces, chopped ham, peppers, mushrooms, or spinach.

THAI-INSPIRED CAMPFIRE CHICKEN

DAIRY-FREE

SERVES 4 TO 6 / PREP TIME: 5 MINUTES / COOK TIME: 30 MINUTES

This meal is a treat to mix it up at the campsite after lots of grilled food. It's perfect for prepping ahead and freezing, and then bringing to the campsite ready to warm and eat.

2 pounds chicken breasts, cut into bite-size cubes

1 (14-ounce) can full-fat coconut milk

½ cup creamy peanut butter

Juice of 1 lime

¼ cup soy sauce

4 garlic cloves, minced

1 bunch scallions

1 teaspoon ground ginger

1 teaspoon ground cumin

2 teaspoons curry powder

½ teaspoon cayenne pepper

Cilantro, for garnish (optional)

PREP AT HOME

1. Combine all the ingredients (except the cilantro and rice) in a gallon-size resealable plastic freezer bag, seal, and lay flat in freezer until ready to use, then transfer to a cooler if you're traveling to your camping area.

2. Chop the cilantro (if using) to use as a garnish and store in a small baggie.

AT THE CAMPSITE

3. Let the meal thaw fully. This is a great meal to have a few days into your camping trip—put it to use keeping your other food cold and then cook it when defrosted.

4. Dump the entire meal into a 12-inch Dutch oven and cover. Simmer on low, suspended over a campfire or sitting on the campfire grate. Remove lid and stir often to avoid sticking to the pan until done, about 30 minutes.
5. Remove the lid and continue cooking until the chicken is cooked through and the sauce reaches the desired consistency.
6. Garnish with cilantro (if using).

TIP: This recipe tastes great served over rice. If you take this route, be sure to cook the rice ahead of time at home so it will be ready to go at the campsite.

SWEET AND SOUR SALMON

DAIRY-FREE, GLUTEN-FREE, NUT-FREE

SERVES 4 TO 6 / PREP TIME: 10 MINUTES / COOK TIME: 10 MINUTES

When I'm in the mood for a slightly lighter meal while camping on hot summer days, salmon is one of my go-tos. This recipe is great even for those who don't particularly like fish, since the honey garlic flavor really shines in this dish.

2 tablespoons honey

1 tablespoon warm water

1½ teaspoons apple cider vinegar

Salt and black pepper

12 ounces salmon, cut into 3 equal-size fillets

Pinch cayenne pepper

1 tablespoon olive oil

3 garlic cloves, minced

½ lemon, cut into wedges

1 tablespoon chopped fresh parsley (optional)

PREP AT HOME

1. Mix the honey, water, apple cider vinegar, and pinch of salt in a leakproof container with a lid.
2. Wrap each salmon fillet in plastic wrap, then in tinfoil, and store in the refrigerator for up to 2 to 3 days, then transfer to a cooler for transporting to the campsite.

AT THE CAMPSITE

3. Sprinkle each fillet, flesh-side up, with a pinch each of salt, black pepper, and cayenne pepper.
4. Heat the olive oil in a cast-iron skillet over high heat.
5. Panfry the salmon, skin-side down first, for about 1 minute. Turn the salmon over and cook for another minute.

6. Turn it over again so the skin side is on the bottom, then add the garlic into the pan and sauté until slightly browned.
7. Add the honey mixture and lemon wedges to the skillet and reduce the sauce. When it's ready, the sauce will be sticky and coat the back of a spoon.
8. Remove the salmon from the pan and top with parsley (if using) and serve immediately.

TIP: Don't have a cast-iron skillet? You can also use a heavy-duty frying pan on a camp stove.

HAWAIIAN DUTCH OVEN CASSEROLE

DAIRY-FREE, GLUTEN-FREE, NUT-FREE

SERVES 4 / **PREP TIME:** 5 MINUTES / **COOK TIME:** 30 MINUTES

Truth be told, I call this a Hawaiian casserole only because it contains pineapple; it's very easy to make and is always a huge hit in my family. And it's a perfect recipe to have on hand for a camping meal since it utilizes so many canned ingredients.

1 (28-ounce) can diced pineapple, drained

1 (28-ounce) can sweet potatoes

1 pound precooked chicken apple sausage, diced

4 tablespoons brown sugar

4 tablespoons butter, cut into pats

1. Spray your Dutch oven with cooking spray or line with tinfoil.
2. Dump the pineapple, sweet potatoes, and diced chicken apple sausage into the Dutch oven and mix well.
3. Sprinkle the brown sugar over the other ingredients, then place the pats of butter on top.
4. Cover with the Dutch oven lid, then place on the grate over hot coals.
5. Cook for 30 minutes, checking and stirring every 10 minutes to avoid burning.

TIP: If you're feeding sausage lovers, add more chicken apple sausage. This recipe also works with kielbasa.

SWEET POTATO AND BLACK BEAN CHILI

NUT-FREE, VEGAN

SERVES 4 TO 6 / PREP TIME: 10 MINUTES / COOK TIME: 35 MINUTES

This chili is great for cooler-weather camping trips when you need a good warming dish! If you love dairy, I recommend topping this chili with some shredded Cheddar cheese or sour cream.

1 medium yellow onion

3 medium sweet potatoes

1 (16-ounce) jar chunky salsa

1 (15-ounce) can black beans, drained and rinsed

2 cups vegetable stock

2 cups water

1 tablespoon chili powder

2 teaspoons ground cumin

½ teaspoon ground cinnamon

Fresh cilantro (optional)

Avocado (optional)

Lime juice (optional)

PREP AT HOME

1. Chop the onion and peel and chop the sweet potatoes into bite-size pieces.

2. Put the onions, sweet potatoes, salsa, black beans, vegetable stock, water, chili powder, cumin, and cinnamon in a resealable plastic freezer bag. Refrigerate or freeze flat, then transfer to a cooler for transporting to the campsite.

AT THE CAMPSITE

3. Thaw the chili if frozen. Dump the entire bag into a Dutch oven pot with a lid (I like to use a Dutch oven on a camp stove).

4. Bring to a boil and then simmer on low, covered, for at least 30 minutes or until the potatoes are soft.

5. Top with optional ingredients and serve.

TERIYAKI-GRILLED STEAK KEBABS

DAIRY-FREE, NUT-FREE

SERVES 6 / PREP TIME: 30 MINUTES / COOK TIME: 15 MINUTES

Teriyaki is a favorite flavor in my family, and it makes for a special treat when camping. Marinating the steak overnight gives it great flavor and tenderness, and makes it easy to pack in the cooler, too. If using wooden skewers, be sure to soak them in water for at least 30 minutes prior to cooking.

1 cup soy sauce

½ cup red wine vinegar

⅔ cup water

1 cup brown sugar

4 garlic cloves, minced

1 teaspoon ground ginger

2 pounds sirloin steak, cut into 1½-inch cubes

1 tablespoon cornstarch

1 green bell pepper cut into 1½-inch pieces

1 red bell pepper cut into 1½-inch pieces

1 onion cut into 1½-inch pieces

1 large pineapple, cut into 1-inch pieces

10 metal or wooden skewers

2 tablespoons sesame seeds

1. In a small bowl, whisk together the soy sauce, red wine vinegar, water, brown sugar, garlic, and ginger until the sugar is dissolved to make a marinade.

2. Add the cubed steak to a large resealable plastic freezer bag along with one-third of the marinade. Let marinate overnight.

3. In a saucepan, add the remaining two-thirds of the marinade and whisk in the cornstarch. Bring to a boil, then reduce heat to low and simmer for 20 minutes or until thickened into a glaze.

4. Cool the glaze, then store in a leakproof container.

5. Store the peppers and onions in a resealable plastic freezer bag.

6. Store the pineapple in a leakproof container.

7. Store the glaze, peppers and onions, and pineapple in the refrigerator until ready to use.

CONTINUED>

AT THE CAMPSITE

8. Build a campfire.

9. Thread the skewers, alternately with steak, peppers, onions, and pineapple.

10. Brush the reserved glaze over each skewer.

11. Grill the skewers for 3 to 4 minutes per side or until desired doneness, brushing with more glaze after each rotation.

12. Remove skewers and let rest for 10 minutes.

13. Sprinkle with sesame seeds.

> **TIP:** You can also pre-skewer these kebabs at home and store in a container for transportation to make this recipe even easier.

CAMPFIRE QUESADILLAS

NUT-FREE, VEGETARIAN

SERVES 6 / **PREP TIME:** 10 MINUTES / **COOK TIME:** 10 MINUTES

Quesadillas are a staple in my home and are a perfect way to sneak in some extra veggies in the middle of gooey cheese. Super fast to make on the campfire grate, quesadillas are also perfect for camping with kids who prefer to eat on the run.

2 teaspoons olive oil

½ medium red onion, thinly sliced

12 button mushrooms, thinly sliced

½ cup frozen corn

¾ cup shredded Cheddar cheese

¾ cup shredded mozzarella cheese

6 large burrito-size flour tortillas

Guacamole (optional)

Salsa (optional)

Sour cream (optional)

PREP AT HOME

1. Heat the olive oil in a medium skillet over medium-high heat and sauté the onion and mushrooms until tender. Add the corn and cook for 4 more minutes.

2. Let cool, then add to a resealable plastic bag.

3. Combine the Cheddar and mozzarella cheeses in a large resealable plastic bag.

4. Store both bags in the refrigerator until ready to use, then transfer to a cooler if you're traveling to your camping area.

CONTINUED>

AT THE CAMPSITE

5. Lay out six pieces of foil and place a tortilla on each piece. Divide half the cheese among the six tortillas.
6. Divide the veggie mixture among the tortillas and top with the remaining half of cheese.
7. Fold tortillas in half along with the tinfoil. Roll up the sides of the foil to seal.
8. Place the packets on the grate and cook for 2 to 3 minutes per side, until the cheese is melted and the tortilla is crisp.
9. Top with guacamole, salsa, and sour cream (if using) and enjoy!

> **TIP:** Cut these quesadillas up into smaller pieces and lay them on a tray for a fun appetizer. Feel free to add steak or chicken to change it up.

MANGO MOJITO CHICKEN

DAIRY-FREE, GLUTEN-FREE, NUT-FREE

SERVES 4 / PREP TIME: 10 MINUTES / COOK TIME: 20 MINUTES

Ring in summer and camping season with this fresh take on chicken. It pairs perfectly with coconut rice (prep at home and just reheat at the campsite). Something about these sunny flavors makes them ideal for summer eating.

2 pounds raw chicken tenders or chicken breasts, cut into strips

2 cups mango chunks

6 fresh mint leaves, very thinly sliced

¼ cup olive oil

2 tablespoons lime juice

1 teaspoon garlic powder

½ teaspoon red pepper flakes

Salt and black pepper

Cilantro, for garnish

PREP AT HOME

1. In a large bowl, combine all the ingredients (except the cilantro) and gently mix.
2. Lay out 4 pieces of foil, approximately 12-by-12 inches.
3. Divide the chicken mixture evenly and place into the center of each piece of foil.
4. Fold the foil over top of the food, then pinch to seal sides.
5. Put the foil packets in a leakproof container and store in the refrigerator until ready to cook, then transfer to a cooler if you're traveling to a campsite.

CONTINUED>

AT THE CAMPSITE

6. Place the foil packets on a campfire grate above small flames or in the coals.

7. Cook for 15 to 20 minutes until the chicken is cooked through.

> **TIP:** If you can't find fresh mango or prefer to make prep for this recipe a little easier, frozen mango chunks will work instead.

ONE-PAN BEEF STROGANOFF

NUT-FREE

SERVES 4 / PREP TIME: 10 MINUTES / COOK TIME: 30 MINUTES

This meal is best made in a heavy-bottom frying pan (I prefer cast iron) on a camp stove. It can be done over a fire also, but it will need to be watched more carefully to avoid burning.

12 ounces mushrooms

½ yellow onion

2 garlic cloves

2 tablespoons butter

1 pound lean ground beef

3 tablespoons flour

4 cups low-sodium beef broth

2 teaspoons dried thyme

2 tablespoons Worcestershire sauce

8 ounces egg noodles

Salt and black pepper

⅓ cup sour cream

PREP AT HOME

1. Wash the mushrooms and slice them into quarters. Store in a resealable plastic bag in the refrigerator.

2. Dice the onion and mince the garlic. Pack together in a second bag and refrigerate.

CAMPSITE COOKING INSTRUCTIONS

3. Melt the butter in a skillet over medium heat.

4. Sauté the mushrooms until tender, 3 to 4 minutes.

5. Add the onion and garlic. Sauté for about 5 minutes until tender and fragrant.

6. Add the ground beef and cook until brown, crumbling the beef as it cooks.

7. Stir in the flour until browned.

CONTINUED>

8. Stir in the beef broth, thyme, Worcestershire sauce, and egg noodles. Let the mixture simmer until the noodles are cooked, 8 to 10 minutes. Add salt and pepper to taste.

9. Once noodles are done, stir in the sour cream until heated through, about 2 minutes. Serve immediately.

CAMPFIRE NACHOS

GLUTEN-FREE, VEGETARIAN

SERVES 4 TO 6 / **PREP TIME:** 10 MINUTES / **COOK TIME:** 15 MINUTES

These layered nachos are a fun dinner to eat with your hands and share with your camping buddies. Don't get hung up on measurements for this one! Just layer, layer, and layer the ingredients until you can't layer anymore. Since everything is already precooked, you're just assembling and melting the cheese, making this an easy dish to prepare by the campfire.

1 bag tortilla chips

1 (14.5-ounce) can fire-roasted tomatoes

1 (15-ounce) can black beans, drained and rinsed

1 (4-ounce) can roasted green chiles

1 (3.8-ounce) can black olive pieces

2 avocados, cubed

3 cups shredded Mexican-blend cheese

4 scallions, sliced

2 limes, cut into wedges

1 cup fresh cilantro, chopped

1. Line your Dutch oven with tinfoil or parchment liner.
2. Spread a layer of tortilla chips, a scoop of the tomatoes, a scoop of the black beans, a bit of the roasted green chiles, a sprinkling of olives, a few cubes of avocado, and about a quarter of the cheese.
3. Repeat these layers until you run out of the ingredients in step 2, about two more layers of each.
4. Add any remaining cheese to the top and sprinkle with the cilantro.
5. Cover with the Dutch oven lid and place on the campfire grill for about 15 minutes to melt the cheese.

BRATS ON BAGUETTES

DAIRY-FREE OPTION, NUT-FREE

SERVES 4 / **PREP TIME:** 5 MINUTES / **COOK TIME:** 25 MINUTES

A little fancier than hot dogs, but still a campfire staple! These brats are made with baguettes for buns and peppers and onions for an kick of flavor.

1 sweet yellow onion

1 red bell pepper

1 yellow bell pepper

1 orange bell pepper

2 tablespoons olive oil

4 bratwurst

4 mini baguettes or pretzel rolls

Mustard and ketchup, for topping (optional)

PREP AT HOME

1. Slice the onion and peppers, place in a resealable plastic bag, and refrigerate until ready to use.

AT THE CAMPSITE

2. Heat the olive oil in a skillet over medium heat. Add the onion and pepper mixtures. Cook for 3 to 4 minutes until they begin to soften.
3. Add the bratwurst to the skillet in an even layer.
4. Stir the veggies and turn the brats often, until they're thoroughly cooked to an internal temperature of 160°F, about 20 minutes. Remove from heat.
5. Slice the baguettes lengthwise. Add the brats and top with onions and peppers. Add the mustard and/or ketchup (if using).

GRILLED PORK LOIN

DAIRY-FREE, GLUTEN-FREE, NUT-FREE

SERVES 4 / **PREP TIME:** 10 MINUTES / **COOK TIME:** 50 MINUTES

Pork grilled over the campfire leaves it with a slightly smoky taste, which my family really loves. The key is to cook it slow without letting it dry out. (The butter in this recipe helps with that.) It's also very helpful to cut your pork loin in half (the long way) to cut down on the cook time.

4 medium potatoes

2 medium sweet onions

2 pounds pork tenderloin

4 tablespoons dried rosemary

4 tablespoons unsalted butter

Salt and black pepper

PREP AT HOME

1. Cut your potatoes and onions into ½-inch slices. Store in a large resealable plastic bag or lidded container and refrigerate until ready to move to your cooler.

2. Cut your pork loin in half the long way. Store in a separate large resealable plastic bag and refrigerate until ready to move to your cooler.

CONTINUED>

AT THE CAMPSITE

3. Start by searing the two pieces of pork loin directly on the fire grate for 1 to 2 minutes per side (this helps lock in the flavor). Set aside.

4. Cut two large pieces of tinfoil and split the pork, potatoes, and onions into two packets.

5. Sprinkle the rosemary on top of the loin and vegetables. Cut the butter into chunks and divide it evenly on top of the loins. Sprinkle with salt and pepper to taste.

6. Cover each loin with a second piece of tinfoil and seal up the edges.

7. Wrap each meal in one more large piece of foil to protect it from burning.

8. Place on a rack above hot coals and cook for about 30 minutes. Check the pork with a food thermometer until it reaches an internal temperature of 145°F. If not yet done, place the packets back on the fire and cook for another 5 to 10 minutes.

9. Remove from fire and let cool for about 10 minutes. Slice the pork loin to serve.

EGG ROLL IN A BOWL

DAIRY-FREE, GLUTEN-FREE

SERVES 6 / **PREP TIME:** 15 MINUTES / **COOK TIME:** 5 TO 10 MINUTES

This meal is one of our favorites at home or at the campsite. It is amazingly delicious and also happens to be low-carb and keto-friendly. You won't even miss the traditional fried egg roll wrapper.

2 tablespoons sesame oil

3 garlic cloves, minced

½ cup diced yellow or white onion

1 pound ground pork

½ teaspoon ground ginger

3 tablespoons gluten-free soy sauce

1 tablespoon rice vinegar

5 scallions, diced

1 (14-ounce) bag coleslaw mix

PREP AT HOME

1. Heat the sesame oil in a large skillet over medium-high heat.
2. Add the garlic and onion and cook until the onions are translucent and the garlic is fragrant.
3. Add the ground pork and ginger. Sauté until the pork is cooked through.
4. Cool and store in a large resealable plastic freezer bag.
5. Combine the soy sauce and rice vinegar in a leak-proof container for transporting.
6. Store the ground pork mixture, scallions, and the soy sauce and vinegar mixture in the refrigerator until ready to use, then transfer to a cooler for transporting to the campsite.

CONTINUED>

AT THE CAMPSITE

7. Reheat the pork mixture over a fire or hot coals until heated through.

8. Add the coleslaw mix and soy sauce and rice wine vinegar mixture.

9. Sauté until the coleslaw is tender. Top with the scallions and serve.

> **TIP:** This meal doesn't keep great as leftovers since the cabbage gets soggy, though it's so good you'll probably rarely have leftovers!

FISH TACOS

GLUTEN-FREE, NUT-FREE

SERVES 4 / PREP TIME: 15 MINUTES / COOK TIME: 10 MINUTES

I am always a little shocked by how quickly my family gobbles up these fish tacos. They are a flavorful light meal that's perfect for warmer weather. These can be made, of course, with fresh-caught fish if preferred.

1½ teaspoons paprika

1½ teaspoons brown sugar

1 teaspoon dried oregano

¾ teaspoon garlic powder

½ teaspoon salt

½ teaspoon ground cumin

½ teaspoon cayenne pepper

4 (6-ounce) tilapia fillets

1 cup shredded carrots

1 handful cilantro, chopped

1 red cabbage, thinly sliced

¼ cup sour cream

Juice of 2 limes

1 tablespoon olive oil

8 (6-inch) corn tortillas

PREP AT HOME

1. Combine the paprika, brown sugar, oregano, garlic powder, salt, cumin, and cayenne pepper in a large resealable plastic bag for seasoning the fish at the campsite.

2. Wrap the tilapia fillets in plastic wrap, then in tinfoil, and refrigerate. Transfer to a cooler before transporting to the campsite.

3. Make the cabbage slaw by mixing the carrots, cilantro, red cabbage, sour cream, and lime juice. Store in another resealable plastic bag and refrigerate, then transfer to a cooler before transporting to camp.

CONTINUED>

AT THE CAMPSITE

4. Heat the olive oil in a large cast-iron skillet over the fire or on the camp stove over medium-high heat.

5. Add the fish fillets to the resealable plastic bag with the seasoning and shake gently to coat evenly.

6. When the oil begins to simmer, add the fish and cook about 3 minutes per side until the fish is lightly browned and flakes easily.

7. Warm the tortillas over the fire slightly, making sure not to burn them. Add a bit of fish to each tortilla and top with the cabbage slaw mix.

TIP: One way to warm the tortillas is to wrap them in tinfoil and lay them on the grate of the campfire. You want them warm but not crunchy for easy wrapping. These tacos pair very well with my No-Cook Southwest Salad (page 90).

CHAPTER 4

SNACKS AND SIDES

If I am really honest with myself, the snacks may just be the most important part of a successful camping trip, especially with kids. Though I am not immune to just grabbing some packaged snacks on the way for simplicity's sake, sometimes it's nice to mix it up (and save some money) with healthy and clean options. The following recipes, which are mostly prepped at home so you can grab and go before you head out, are my go-to favorites.

CONTINUED>

CONTINUED

GARLIC BUTTER CAMPFIRE CORN

GLUTEN-FREE, VEGETARIAN

SERVES 4 / **PREP TIME:** 10 MINUTES / **COOK TIME:** 15 MINUTES

This recipe is so simple but a huge favorite for around-the-campfire eating. If you have corn lovers you are cooking for, I highly recommend doubling this recipe!

2 tablespoons butter, softened

1 tablespoon minced garlic

¼ cup chopped fresh chives

¼ teaspoon salt

¼ teaspoon black pepper

4 medium corncobs, husked

PREP AT HOME

1. Combine the butter, garlic, chives, salt, and pepper in a small bowl.
2. Rub the flavored butter on the corn, then wrap each one tightly in foil.
3. Refrigerate until ready to hit the campsite.

AT THE CAMPSITE

4. Cook the wrapped corncobs about 4 to 6 inches over hot coals for 15 minutes, turning occasionally.
5. Let cool slightly before carefully unwrapping.

TIP: Butter should be soft but not melted when prepping this recipe. It's easier to rub on the corn when it's not totally melted. I love to throw this corn on the grate above coals while cooking the Vegetable Medley (page 84).

VEGETABLE MEDLEY

NUT-FREE, VEGAN

SERVES 4 / **PREP TIME:** 10 MINUTES / **COOK TIME:** 30 MINUTES

These veggies cooked in foil packets are by far my favorite way to eat healthy while camping. They are perfect on their own as a snack or on the side of a main meat dish.

1 medium zucchini

3 medium carrots

12 ounces baby potatoes

1 large red onion

3 or 4 whole garlic cloves

4 tablespoons olive oil

¼ teaspoon black pepper

1 teaspoon paprika

1½ tablespoons dried oregano

1 teaspoon salt

1 teaspoon garlic powder

1 tablespoon dried rosemary (optional)

PREP AT HOME

1. Slice the zucchini and carrots and place in a large resealable plastic bag.
2. Quarter the baby potatoes and add to the bag.
3. Cut the onion into rings and add to the bag.
4. Add the whole garlic cloves to the bag.
5. Drizzle the olive oil into the bag, seal it with air in it, and shake to coat the veggies.
6. Combine the pepper, paprika, oregano, salt, garlic, and rosemary (if using) in a small bowl and mix well.
7. Add the spice mixture to the bag of veggies and olive oil, seal it, and toss well.
8. Refrigerate the veggies until ready to cook.

9. At the campsite, divide the veggies among four sheets of tinfoil.

10. Fold the tinfoil into a packet and seal the edges tightly.

11. Cook on a campfire grate until the desired doneness, 20 to 30 minutes.

> **TIP:** These veggies are so easy to prep and then leave in your cooler until you want them. The longer they sit refrigerated (up to 3 days), the better they marinate in the flavors.

OATMEAL PEANUT BUTTER ENERGY BARS

DAIRY-FREE, VEGAN

SERVES 4 TO 6 / PREP TIME: 10 MINUTES, PLUS 2 HOURS TO CHILL

Just like the Get-Hiking-More Trail Bars (page 106), these Oatmeal Peanut Butter Energy Bars are definitely ones you will want to make ahead of time and bring with you. Freeze them until you're ready to go and store them in the cooler for some quick energy whenever you need it. I love that I know exactly what is in these, and I can feel good about making them for my family.

1 cup mixed nuts (pecans, walnuts, cashews, almonds, etc.)

1 cup old-fashioned oats

½ cup dried cranberries

2 tablespoons chia seeds

1 teaspoon ground cinnamon

Pinch ground nutmeg

½ cup peanut butter

¼ cup honey

1 teaspoon pure vanilla extract

1. In a food processor or blender, pulse the nuts until ground with some small chunks. Add the oats, dried cranberries, chia seeds, cinnamon, and nutmeg. Pulse lightly to combine.

2. Add the peanut butter, honey, and vanilla to the mixture and pulse until all the ingredients are well combined.

3. Press the mixture into an 8-inch square baking dish in an even layer. Cover and refrigerate for at least 2 hours or until firm.

4. When the mixture is firm, use a knife to cut it into bars. Wrap them individually in plastic wrap or store in an airtight container. Freeze or refrigerate until ready to use.

TIP: It's important to not blend the nuts until they become a paste in the first step. You want some chunks to add texture to the bars.

CHEESY GARLIC POTATOES

GLUTEN-FREE, NUT-FREE, VEGETARIAN

SERVES 6 / PREP TIME: 50 MINUTES / COOK TIME: 15 MINUTES

These Cheesy Garlic Potatoes are the perfect comfort food to eat around the campfire. Even better, they're easy to prep at home so you can cut down your work at the campsite.

6 potatoes, thinly sliced

1 cup diced red bell pepper

¼ cup diced onion

1 tablespoon minced garlic

1 (16-ounce) package mini smoked sausages

2 tablespoons cold butter, thinly sliced

¼ cup grated Parmesan cheese

½ cup shredded mozzarella cheese

¾ cup shredded Cheddar cheese

Salt and black pepper

PREP AT HOME

1. Preheat the oven to 350°F.

2. Wrap the potatoes in foil individually, place them in the oven, and cook for 45 minutes.

3. Remove the foil and let cool, then place the potatoes in a large resealable plastic bag or sealed container for transporting to the campsite.

AT THE CAMPSITE

4. Cut 2 large pieces of heavy-duty tinfoil, about 12-by-12 inches.

5. Lay the sheets side by side and pinch the seam to create one large sheet. Spray the top layer with cooking spray.

6. Spread the potatoes on the foil, leaving about 3 inches around the perimeter so you can close up the foil.
7. Scatter the bell pepper, onion, garlic, and sausages over the potatoes.
8. Top with the butter.
9. Sprinkle the Parmesan, mozzarella, and Cheddar cheeses on top.
10. Add salt and black pepper to taste.
11. Fold up the foil packet and seal the edges tightly. Use another sheet of foil over top if necessary to close the packet.
12. Place directly on hot coals and cook until potatoes are done, 15 minutes.

TIP: The thinner the potatoes are sliced, the faster they will cook. If you prefer them a little thicker, just pre-cook them before slicing.

NO-COOK SOUTHWEST SALAD

DAIRY-FREE OPTION, GLUTEN-FREE, VEGETARIAN

SERVES 6 TO 8 / PREP TIME: 10 MINUTES, PLUS 10 MINUTES TO REST

This salad can be made up to two days before eating, so it's a great prep-ahead recipe. Make this two to three days before you need it so the flavors have time to mingle. It yields a large amount, so I like to make a batch of it if I'm making food for a crowd. The queso fresco adds a nice touch, but it is not necessary if you prefer it to be dairy-free.

FOR THE DRESSING

Zest and juice of 1 lime

2 tablespoons olive oil

1 tablespoon honey

1 teaspoon ground cumin

⅛ teaspoon cayenne pepper

Salt and black pepper

FOR THE SALAD

2 cups frozen or canned corn

¼ cup red onion, finely chopped

1 (15-ounce) can black beans, drained and rinsed

3 ounces queso fresco, crumbled

1 small bunch fresh cilantro, chopped

TO MAKE THE DRESSING

1. In a mixing bowl, combine the lime zest, lime juice, olive oil, honey, cumin, cayenne pepper, and salt and black pepper to taste. Combine well.

TO MAKE THE SALAD

2. In a large bowl, combine the corn, red onion, black beans, queso fresco, and cilantro.
3. Toss with the dressing and let sit for 30 minutes or more to let the flavors marinate, then serve or refrigerate until ready to use.

TIP: Though you can certainly eat this salad on its own, it tastes amazing with corn chips as a dip, too.

LEMON-PARMESAN BROCCOLI FOIL PACKS

NUT-FREE, VEGETARIAN

SERVES 4 / PREP TIME: 5 MINUTES / COOK TIME: 15 MINUTES

Getting enough nutrients while camping can be a little tough if you don't plan for healthy meals. I love to have nutrient-rich broccoli ready to go, and this recipe combining lemon and Parmesan will make anyone a broccoli lover. I usually dump all the packets into one large bowl after cooking for easy serving, but you certainly can eat it right from the foil.

1 (12-ounce) bag frozen broccoli florets

1 tablespoon lemon juice

1 tablespoon olive oil

½ teaspoon salt

¼ teaspoon black pepper

¼ cup shredded Parmesan cheese

PREP AT HOME

1. Combine the broccoli, lemon juice, olive oil, salt, and pepper in a resealable plastic bag. Shake to combine well. Refrigerate or freeze until ready to cook.

AT THE CAMPSITE

2. At the campsite, tear off four 12-inch-long sheets of heavy-duty foil. Spray with cooking spray.

3. Divide the broccoli among the four pieces of foil. Sprinkle with Parmesan cheese, dividing evenly among the 4 packets.

4. Make a foil packet by folding the foil over itself and then pinching each of the edges to seal. Leave a small opening for steaming.

5. Cook for 20 to 25 minutes or until the broccoli is heated through and tender, then serve.

TIP: Love lemon pepper? Sub out the pepper with lemon pepper for an extra punch!

DUTCH OVEN POTATOES

GLUTEN-FREE, NUT-FREE

SERVES 6 / **PREP TIME:** 15 MINUTES / **COOK TIME:** 25 MINUTES

These Dutch oven potatoes just may become your new favorite go-to side dish, camping or otherwise. They're hearty, easy to make, and pair well with just about any entrée.

½ pound bacon

2½ pounds Russet potatoes

1 small onion, chopped

¼ cup fresh
parsley, chopped

1 tablespoon seasoned salt

Black pepper

½ cup water

2 tablespoons butter, cut
into small pieces

2 cups shredded Cheddar
cheese (optional)

PREP AT HOME

1. Cut the bacon into 1-inch pieces. Store in a small resealable plastic bag.

2. Peel and cut the potatoes into bite-size chunks and put them in a large resealable plastic bag with the onion, parsley, and salt and pepper to taste and refrigerate until ready to use, then transfer to a cooler for transporting to the campsite.

AT THE CAMPSITE

3. In a Dutch oven placed on the fire grill grate, cook the bacon until crisp.

4. Add the bag of potatoes, water, and the butter. Stir to combine.

5. Cover the Dutch oven and cook until the potatoes are browned and tender, about 20 minutes.

6. Add the Cheddar cheese (if using) and let melt. Serve warm.

TIP: It's important to watch the potatoes closely when you cook over a fire. I recommend turning the Dutch oven a quarter turn every 5 minutes to prevent burning.

GLUTEN-FREE CAMPFIRE BEANS

DAIRY-FREE, GLUTEN-FREE, NUT-FREE

SERVES 4 / PREP TIME: 4 TO 6 HOURS / COOK TIME: 15 TO 25 MINUTES

This recipe is loaded with protein and fiber and can easily be used as a main dish or a side dish. I recommend cooking this at home beforehand and then reheating at the campsite. Make a big batch, freeze it in smaller containers, and bring it out for each camping trip.

3 pounds ground beef

1 pound bacon

1 cup chopped onion

3 (16-ounce) cans gluten-free baked beans

2 (16-ounce) cans gluten-free dark red kidney beans

1 (16-ounce) can gluten-free butter beans

1 cup ketchup

½ cup brown sugar

3 tablespoons white vinegar

1 teaspoon salt

1 teaspoon black pepper

PREP AT HOME

1. Chop the bacon into bite-size pieces. In a skillet over medium-high heat, brown the beef and bacon together. Drain the fat.

2. Place the bacon and beef along with all the other ingredients in a 7-quart slow cooker, and stir well.

3. Cover and cook on low for 4 to 6 hours.

4. Cool the beans and pack in airtight containers. Freeze or refrigerate until ready to use, then transfer to a cooler for transporting to the campsite.

5. Place the beans in a Dutch oven and simmer over the campfire for 15 minutes if thawed, or 25 minutes if frozen.

> **TIP:** Bacon is naturally gluten-free, but some brands do contain trace amounts due to cross contamination in factories. Look for bacon marked "gluten-free" on the packaging to be sure.

QUINOA AND BLACK BEAN SALAD

DAIRY-FREE, NUT-FREE, VEGAN

SERVES 4 TO 6 / PREP TIME: 10 MINUTES, PLUS 1 HOUR TO CHILL

This salad is fantastically refreshing on a hot day, and perfect for consuming more vegetables on camping trips. Quinoa is chock-full of protein to keep the whole family energized. It is best served chilled, so I usually make it a couple of days before I need it and let the flavors marinate.

2 tablespoons olive oil

¼ cup lime juice

1 tablespoon apple cider vinegar

1 garlic clove, minced

1 teaspoon ground cumin

1 teaspoon fine sea salt

2 cups quinoa, cooked according to package directions and kept warm

1 red bell pepper, chopped

½ red onion, finely chopped

3 scallions, chopped

1 (15-ounce) can black beans, drained and rinsed

1 cup corn

½ cup freshly chopped cilantro

3 avocados (optional)

1. In a large bowl, combine the olive oil, lime juice, apple cider vinegar, garlic, cumin, and salt in a large bowl to make a dressing.
2. Add the warm quinoa, bell pepper, onion, scallions, black beans, and corn. Toss until well combined.
3. Stir in the cilantro.
4. Chill for at least an hour before serving or packing to take camping. Cube and add the avocados (if using) immediately before serving.

STORAGE TIP: This recipe, without avocados, will stay fresh in the fridge for up to 5 days.

BACON-WRAPPED BRUSSELS SPROUTS

DAIRY-FREE, GLUTEN-FREE, NUT-FREE

SERVES 4 / PREP TIME: 30 MINUTES / COOK TIME: 10 MINUTES

If you think you don't like Brussels sprouts, you probably haven't tried them with bacon! These sprouts grill perfectly over a fire grate and are a camping staple in my family. They take a little time to skewer (either wood or metal ones will work), so I highly recommend doing all the prep work at home.

1 tablespoon olive oil

⅓ cup soy sauce

¼ teaspoon black pepper

¼ teaspoon garlic powder

16 Brussels sprouts

8 slices bacon

PREP AT HOME

1. In a small bowl, whisk together the olive oil, soy sauce, pepper, and garlic powder.

2. Cut the Brussels sprouts in half lengthwise, and place in a large resealable plastic bag with the olive oil mixture to marinate for 20 minutes.

3. To skewer, poke one end of a piece of bacon through the skewer, add a Brussels sprout half, then fold the bacon over the sprout and onto the skewer. Repeat with 3 more sprout halves, ending with bacon.

4. Place the skewers in foil or an airtight container and refrigerate until ready to cook, then transfer to a cooler for transporting to the campsite.

5. Set the fire grill about 6 inches above the flame. Watch the fire carefully during cooking as dripping bacon grease may cause the fire to spark.

6. Grill the skewers for 5 minutes, flip, then grill for an additional 4 to 5 minutes or until the bacon is crisp and the Brussels sprouts are charred. Remove from grill.

> **TIP:** Brussels sprouts are harder to skewer if they aren't cut in half, which also allows them to cook faster. Make sure to let the skewers cool slightly after removing them from the fire—the metal skewers will be hot! If using wooden skewers, be sure to soak them first for at least 30 minutes to avoid burning them.

HAWAIIAN MACARONI SALAD

NUT-FREE

SERVES 6 / PREP TIME: 10 MINUTES, PLUS 1 HOUR TO CHILL

This salad always gets gobbled up by anyone who loves Hawaiian flavors—in this case, ham and pineapple! It's a great dish to prep ahead and bring to the campsite. You can also make this with gluten-free noodles if desired.

½ pound elbow macaroni, cooked and rinsed in cold water

1 (20-ounce) can pineapple chunks, drained (reserve ½ cup of the liquid)

2 cups cubed cooked ham

½ cup shredded carrot

¼ cup scallion

½ cup mayonnaise

¼ cup plain Greek yogurt

1 tablespoon apple cider vinegar

1 tablespoon sugar

1. In a large bowl (with a lid if possible for easy transportation), combine the macaroni, pineapple chunks, ham, carrot, and scallion.

2. In a small bowl, whisk together the reserved pineapple juice, mayonnaise, Greek yogurt, apple cider vinegar, and sugar.

3. Poor the pineapple dressing over the noodle mixture and toss to coat.

4. Refrigerate for about 1 hour to let the flavors meld. Serve cold.

> **TIP:** Be sure not to overcook your pasta or it will be mushy when added to the salad. I recommend cooking al dente.

WATERMELON FETA SALAD WITH CUCUMBER AND BLUEBERRIES

GLUTEN-FREE

SERVES 8+ / PREP TIME: 10 MINUTES, PLUS 1 TO 2 HOURS TO CHILL

If you're looking for a light salad, this unique blend of flavors is perfect for pairing with a campfire meal. This recipe yields a large amount, making it perfect for a big group or leftovers for a couple-day camping trip.

Juice and zest of 3 limes

5 tablespoons olive oil

Salt and black pepper

1 large watermelon, cut into 1-inch cubes

2 pints fresh blueberries

2 cucumbers peeled, halved lengthwise, and cut into ½-inch pieces

8 ounces feta cheese, crumbled

1. In a small bowl, combine the lime juice, lime zest, olive oil, and salt and pepper to taste.
2. In a large bowl (preferably with a lid for easy transportation), toss together the watermelon, blueberries, and cucumber.
3. Sprinkle the feta cheese over the fruit and drizzle with the lime dressing.
4. Chill for 1 to 2 hours before serving.

> **TIP:** This salad can be made the day ahead but is best eaten within 48 hours. If you aren't a huge fan of feta cheese, use 4 ounces instead of 8, or eliminate it altogether.

LEMON-DILL ASPARAGUS AND GREEN BEANS

GLUTEN-FREE

SERVES 4 / **PREP TIME:** 10 MINUTES / **COOK TIME:** 15 MINUTES

Trying to add more green veggies to your camping meal plan? This is a perfect side dish to go with just about anything. Easy to prep, this dish also cooks quickly and is ready to eat in about 20 minutes.

1 pound green beans

1 pound asparagus

½ lemon

1 tablespoon butter, thinly sliced

½ teaspoon dried dill weed

Salt

¼ cup pistachio pieces (optional)

PREP AT HOME

1. Wash and trim the green beans and asparagus and place into a 9-by-11-inch foil pan.

2. Squeeze the lemon over the beans and asparagus. Spread the butter slices over the greens. Sprinkle the dill and salt (to taste) on top.

3. Cut the squeezed lemon into wedges and add to the foil pan with the vegetables.

4. Cover with the foil lid and refrigerate until ready to cook.

5. If using pistachios, add them to the pan with the vegetables right before cooking and cover with the foil lid.

6. Place the foil pan on the grate of a cooking fire. Cook for about 10 minutes until done.

7. Remove the lid and continue cooking for 1 to 2 minutes while tossing to crisp up the asparagus and green beans.

GET-HIKING-MORE TRAIL BARS

DAIRY-FREE OPTION, NUT-FREE, VEGETARIAN

SERVES 4 TO 6 / **PREP TIME:** 10 MINUTES / **COOK TIME:** 30 MINUTES

This recipe will need to be made before you leave for camping (a double batch is a really good idea!) and stored in an airtight container, which makes it the perfect grab-and-go snack for outdoor adventures. These trail bars can also be frozen for up to three weeks. I like to make big batches and freeze them to use for our camping trips.

1¾ cups rolled oats

2 tablespoons granulated sugar

¼ cup dried apricots

¼ cup raisins

3 tablespoons ground flaxseed

¼ cup unsalted sunflower seeds

¼ cup unsweetened shredded coconut

⅔ cup cooked quinoa

2 tablespoons chia seeds

¼ teaspoon baking soda

¼ cup honey

¼ cup unsalted butter, melted (or use ½ cup coconut oil instead of ¼ cup)

¼ cup melted coconut oil

½ teaspoon vanilla extract

Pinch salt

1. Preheat the oven to 350°F.

2. Pulverize half the oats in a food processor or blender until the oats are the consistency of a coarse flour.

3. Add the remaining oats and all other dry ingredients. Process until the raisins and apricots are in small bits. The mixture may begin to stick together at this point.

4. Pour in the honey, butter (if using), coconut oil, and vanilla and pulse to combine.

5. Remove the mixture from the food processor and place in a bowl.

6. Line a baking sheet with parchment paper. Divide the oat mixture into two halves.

7. Take one half of the mixture and press into the pan in a rectangular shape. Repeat with the other half on the other side of the pan. Leave space between each section.

8. Place into the preheated oven and bake for 13 to 16 minutes or until evenly browned. Remove from oven. Lower the oven temperature to 250°F.

9. Cut the oblong slabs into bars and leave in the pan with space between each bar.

CONTINUED>

10. Return to the oven and bake for another 15 minutes. Remove and let cool.
11. Store in an airtight container or bag for 4 days at room temperature, or up to 3 weeks in the freezer.

> **TIP:** Parchment paper makes these bars so much easier to cut up and remove from the pan—don't skip this step!

CHAPTER 5

DESSERTS AND DRINKS

Believe it or not, there are many more delicious options for camping desserts beyond the traditional s'mores. In this chapter I've gathered my favorite ways to treat myself with classic favorites, new desserts with a twist, and special drinks.

BANANA BOAT SAMOAS

VEGETARIAN

SERVES 6 / PREP TIME: 10 MINUTES / COOK TIME: 5 MINUTES

This dessert is the perfect cross between a s'more and a banana split, and is a great dessert for kids to make themselves. You just split a banana in half, stuff it with goodness, wrap it in the oh-so-necessary tinfoil, and throw it in hot coals or on a fire grate. Store your desired toppings in individual snack-size plastic bags to make assembly at the campfire a breeze.

6 large bananas

1 cup large chocolate chips (I like to use dairy-free dark chocolate)

1 cup caramel sauce

½ cup toasted coconut

OPTIONAL TOPPINGS

Mini marshmallows

Crumbled graham crackers

Strawberries

Chocolate hazelnut spread

Peanut butter

M&Ms

1. Slice your bananas, still in the peel, down the middle lengthwise, so the knife just grazes the peel on the other side.

2. Pull the banana slightly away from the peel so you have space to do some stuffing.

3. Add the chocolate chips in a line down the middle of the banana.

4. Drizzle a thin line of caramel sauce over the chocolate chips, the sprinkle the toasted coconut on top. Add any additional toppings you like.

5. Close up the banana in its peel and wrap it tightly in tinfoil.

6. Place the banana boat in hot coals or, if you have flames, on a fire grate.
7. Cook until the chocolate inside is just melted, about 5 minutes.
8. Let cool slightly, then open up and enjoy with a spoon!

RECIPE TIP: Though this recipe is the version that my family prefers, don't be limited by just one flavor! Feel free to offer a variety of toppings and let campers build their own.

ORANGE CHOCOLATE CAMPFIRE BROWNIES

DAIRY-FREE, NUT-FREE, VEGAN

SERVES 5 / **PREP TIME:** 10 MINUTES / **COOK TIME:** 15 MINUTES

I first came across this recipe in a silly teenage novel about a summer at camp. I couldn't wait to make it on my own for myself, and then, later, my own family. Since these brownies can be a little messy, it's best to scoop out the oranges at home and then cook and eat them within 24 hours or so.

5 large oranges

1 box brownie mix

PREP AT HOME

1. Cut off the very top of the oranges and scoop out the insides. Try to slice the oranges a bit while inside the peel to make it easier to scoop. Set aside the oranges and their tops to bring with you camping.

2. Mix the brownie batter according to package directions in a resealable plastic bag and store in the refrigerator until ready to use.

AT THE CAMPSITE

3. Pour some of the brownie mix into each of the oranges so they are about three-quarters full.

4. Replace the tops on the oranges.

5. Wrap the oranges in heavy-duty tinfoil. Set the wrapped orange in the middle of another sheet of tinfoil, pull the sides up, and twist to make a foil handle.

6. Set the oranges in the coals of your fire and cook for 10 minutes. Check the batter for doneness, then cook for another 5 to 10 minutes if necessary before checking again.

7. Remove from fire, let cool slightly, and eat warm.

TIP: The trick to this recipe is to not let the oranges tip over (hence the handy dandy handle) and then to cook them in hot coals with no flames. The time for cooking varies depending on how large the oranges are, how much you scooped out of them, and the thickness of the peel. Be ready to watch them carefully and check often.

STRAWBERRIES AND CREAM CINNAMON DOUGH BOYS

NUT-FREE, VEGETARIAN

MAKES 6 / PREP TIME: 5 MINUTES / COOK TIME: 5 MINUTES

These are a super fun and interactive campfire treat that can be modified as needed with different fruits and fillings. You can use regular sticks if you need to, but these cook much better on 1½-inch dowels. We made a few of them just for this dessert and keep them in a safe place until we're ready to use them.

2 cups sliced strawberries

¼ cup brown sugar

2 tablespoons ground cinnamon

Butter, for greasing the dowels

1 (6-count) can instant biscuits

Whipped cream, for topping

PREP AT HOME

1. In a mixing bowl, combine the strawberries, brown sugar, and cinnamon.
2. Transfer the strawberry mixture to a large resealable plastic bag and refrigerate until ready to use.

AT THE CAMPSITE

3. Butter the end of each ½-inch wooden dowel (6 in total).
4. Take a biscuit and carefully lengthen it into a rope-like shape. Wrap it around the length of the dowel and seal the end so there are no holes in the dough, making a tube.

5. Carefully roast over the campfire for about 5 minutes until the tube comes easily off the stick (careful, it will be hot!).
6. Once slightly cooled, evenly divide the strawberry mixture into each tube, then top with whipped cream and enjoy.

> **TIP:** The thinner you can get the dough on the stick, the faster it will cook (and a lesser chance of them being underdone in the middle).

DUTCH OVEN CHERRY COBBLER

VEGETARIAN

SERVES 6 / PREP TIME: 10 MINUTES / COOK TIME: 20 MINUTES

My mom made this cobbler every time we camped when I was a child, and it is still one of my very favorite desserts. She made hers with lemon-lime soda. I like to make mine with flavored seltzer in an effort to cut down on the sweetness, and it's perfect. It's also easy to keep these ingredients on hand in your camp kitchen for whenever you're craving cobbler!

2 (21-ounce) cans cherry pie filling

1 (12-ounce) can flavored seltzer water

1 package yellow cake mix

Whipped cream or ice cream (optional)

1. Line a 6-quart Dutch oven with tinfoil.
2. Dump both cans of the pie filling into the bottom of the Dutch oven.
3. Mix the seltzer water with the cake mix (I often do this in a resealable plastic bag before adding to the Dutch oven, and combine with my hands). Dump the cake batter on top of the pie filling and spread evenly.
4. Set the Dutch oven on coals.
5. Add the lid to the Dutch oven and cover in coals.

6. Cook for about 20 minutes, rotating the oven about halfway through, until the cake is golden brown.

7. Top with whipped cream or ice cream (if using) before serving.

> **TIP:** This recipe works great with *any* pie filling. I recommend blueberry, apple, and raspberry. You can also use fresh fruit instead of pie filling (just add a few tablespoons of butter to the top before cooking). For easy cleanup, you can dump the cake mix into the Dutch oven and then top it with the soda. However, be sure to mix lightly with a spoon so no dry pockets remain.

DUTCH OVEN BANANA BREAD

VEGETARIAN

SERVES 4 / **PREP TIME:** 5 MINUTES / **COOK TIME:** 30 MINUTES

This dessert (which also makes a fantastic breakfast or snack) is such a treat for around the campfire. For this recipe you need *just* hot coals that are burned down well. You want it to cook low and gentle. Don't worry if you accidentally burn the bottom of the bread. It happens sometimes! When it does, I just scoop out the good parts with a spoon, and it's always delicious.

1½ cups flour

1 cup brown sugar

2 teaspoons ground cinnamon

1 teaspoon baking soda

Pinch salt

4 ripe bananas, peeled

½ cup softened butter

1 teaspoon vanilla extract

1 egg

Chopped walnuts, for topping (optional)

Chocolate chips, for topping (optional)

PREP AT HOME

1. Mix the flour, brown sugar, cinnamon, baking soda, and salt together in a large resealable plastic bag.

2. In a second large resealable plastic bag, mix the bananas, butter, vanilla, and egg. Mash together until the mixture is well combined, then refrigerate until ready to use.

AT THE CAMPSITE

3. Lay a fire and burn down until just hot coals.

4. Line the Dutch oven with parchment paper or tinfoil.

5. Add the dry ingredients to the banana mixture and mix well. If using the walnuts and/or chocolate chips, add them in and mix until just combined. I think it works best to close the resealable plastic bag and carefully squish it all together with your hands.

6. Pour the batter into the Dutch oven and cover with the lid. Make a ring of 5 coals (or wood equivalent) and place the Dutch oven on top. Place 15 coals (or wood equivalent) on the lid.

7. Cook for about 30 minutes. Rotate the Dutch oven every 10 minutes so it cooks evenly. After 30 minutes, check for doneness (by doing the toothpick test or using a knife) and bake a little longer if needed.

8. Remove from the coals and cool for a few minutes, then cut into wedges and serve.

TIP: Though it's not required, this recipe does best using a parchment liner in the Dutch oven instead of foil. It's cheap and makes popping out the bread very easy.

GRILLED CARAMEL APPLE CRUNCH

NUT-FREE, VEGETARIAN

SERVES 4 / PREP TIME: 10 MINUTES / COOK TIME: 15 MINUTES

I personally love caramel apples for dessert—and I love them even more around the campfire. The mix of apples with the caramel and the crunch from the granola make this the perfect blend of flavors.

4 large apples, diced into ¼-inch cubes, divided

4 tablespoons butter, cubed, divided

Ground cinnamon, for sprinkling

½ cup caramel sauce, divided

1 cup granola (any flavor), divided

Ice cream or whipped cream (optional)

1. Build a fire and let it burn down a bit.

2. Tear off 8 (8-inch) square pieces of tinfoil for each packet.

3. Set aside four of the tinfoil pieces. On the four remaining pieces:

   Place 1 chopped apple in the center of the foil.

   Add 1 tablespoon of cubed butter on top of the apples.

   Sprinkle with cinnamon.

   Drizzle 2 tablespoons of the caramel sauce.

   Top with ¼ cup of granola.

4. Top each loaded square with another square of tinfoil and roll up the edges so it is well sealed.

5. Place over coals (or on a fire grate if you still have flames) for 10 to 15 minutes, until apples are soft.

6. Remove from fire. Be cautious as you open the packets because the steam escaping will be very hot.

7. Serve warm with whipped cream or ice cream (if using).

TIP: You can easily make this recipe on a grill if you don't have access to a campfire.

BAKED APPLES

GLUTEN-FREE, VEGETARIAN

SERVES 4 / PREP TIME: 10 MINUTES / COOK TIME: 10 MINUTES

This is another super easy recipe that is so yummy around the fire. It's a perfect treat that tastes similar to apple pie but without the crust.

1 tablespoon
ground cinnamon

¼ cup brown sugar

¼ cup chopped
pecans (optional)

4 Granny Smith
apples, cored

Cool Whip (optional)

1. In a small bowl, mix together the cinnamon, brown sugar, and pecans (if using).
2. Divide the cinnamon, sugar, and pecan mixture evenly among the 4 apples and stuff the cores.
3. Wrap each apple in a large piece of heavy-duty tinfoil, bringing the ends to the top and twisting the extra foil into a handle.
4. Place the apples, handle-side up, in the coals of a campfire and let cook for 5 to 10 minutes until softened.
5. Remove and unwrap. Let cool slightly, cut into slices, and enjoy warm with Cool Whip (if using).

> **TIP:** When I make this at home I like to top it with ice cream but that can be a bit tricky to transport, which is why I included Cool Whip instead. Be sure to freeze it before leaving home to keep it as cold as possible.

ORANGE CINNAMON ROLLS

DAIRY-FREE, NUT-FREE

SERVES 4 / PREP TIME: 5 MINUTES / COOK TIME: 30 MINUTES

If you're not into the Orange Chocolate Campfire Brownies on page 114, these cinnamon rolls are a great sweet treat or a special breakfast option. And they're cooked right inside the orange peel for easy cleanup!

6 large oranges

1 (12-ounce) can cinnamon roll dough with icing

PREP AT HOME

1. Cut off the very top of the oranges and scoop out the insides. Try to slice the oranges a bit while inside the peel to make it easier to scoop. Place the oranges and their tops in resealable plastic bags to bring with you camping.

AT THE CAMPSITE

2. Prepare your campfire by placing a rack above the glowing embers.

3. Open the can of cinnamon rolls and insert one roll into each orange, making sure it is pressed all the way to the bottom.

CONTINUED>

4. Replace the tops of the oranges and then wrap each one tightly with tinfoil.

5. Place the wrapped oranges on top of the grill over the embers.

6. Cook for 25 to 30 minutes until the cinnamon rolls are cooked through.

7. Remove from heat and let cool for 5 minutes. Unwrap the foil and take the top off the orange. Drizzle icing onto each cinnamon roll and serve warm.

> **TIP:** You can easily make this recipe on a grill or in a 375°F oven if you don't have access to a campfire.

ROCKY ROAD CAMPFIRE CONES

VEGETARIAN

SERVES 4 / **PREP TIME:** 5 MINUTES / **COOK TIME:** 5 MINUTES

Love s'mores but hate the mess? This is a fun way to have a warm camping treat without a gooey face and fingers. This is just one recipe option—feel free to stuff the cones with anything sweet that sounds good to you!

4 waffle cones

1 cup mixed nuts, divided

1 cup mini marshmallows, divided

1 cup peanut butter chocolate cups, chopped, divided

1. Build a fire and let it burn down to coals.
2. Fill each waffle cone with the following:
   ¼ cup of mixed nuts
   ¼ cup of mini marshmallows
   ¼ cup of peanut butter chocolate cups
3. Wrap each cone in foil and grill to warm the ingredients, about 5 minutes.
4. Remove from fire and carefully unwrap the top of the cone first. Enjoy!

TIP: You can easily make this recipe on a grill if you don't have access to a campfire.

MOUNTAIN MARGARITA

GLUTEN-FREE, NUT-FREE, VEGAN

MAKES 1 / **PREP TIME:** 5 MINUTES

Iced drinks while camping are a necessity for winding down after a busy day, and perfect for car camping. This quick margarita is my favorite drink recipe to make by the campfire.

1 (12-ounce) can orange soda

1½ ounces tequila

½ lime

Ice

Rock salt (optional)

1. Mix the orange soda, tequila, squeeze of lime, and ice in a sealed jar or cocktail shaker and shake.

2. Slide the lime wedge around the rim of your cup, then dip in the rock salt (if using).

3. Pour the margarita into your prepared cup and enjoy!

MEXICAN HOT CHOCOLATE

NUT-FREE, VEGETARIAN

MAKES ABOUT 32 CUPS / **PREP TIME:** 5 MINUTES / **COOK TIME:** 5 MINUTES

Skip the packets of hot chocolate and make your own! This powdered hot chocolate tastes amazing and makes a large batch. The flavor is quite rich, so I think about 2½ tablespoons of powder per drink is just enough to get great flavor without it being overpowering. That said, feel free to add more or less to your taste.

2 cups powdered instant milk

1 cup powdered sugar

1 cup brown sugar

1 cup dark cocoa powder

1 teaspoon salt

2 cups semisweet chocolate chips

1 tablespoon cinnamon

½ teaspoon cayenne pepper

Marshmallows (optional)

Whipped cream (optional)

PREP AT HOME

1. Add all the ingredients together (except the toppings) in a blender or food processor. Pulse several times until everything is mixed together and the chocolate chips are in pieces.

2. Store in a large resealable plastic bag or airtight container until ready to use.

AT THE CAMPSITE

3. Add 2½ tablespoons of mixture to a cup of hot water.

4. Mix until the chocolate chip pieces are melted.

5. Top with marshmallows or whipped cream (if using) and enjoy!

ROOT BEER FLOATS

NUT-FREE, VEGETARIAN

SERVES 4 / PREP TIME: 5 MINUTES

Yes, it *is* possible to have root beer floats while camping! This recipe uses Cool Whip instead of ice cream because it doesn't have to stay frozen—just cold—so it's much easier to transport! This refreshing, sweet drink will hit the spot while camping.

1 (16-ounce) container Cool Whip, frozen

4 (12-ounce) cans root beer

1. Scoop desired amount of Cool Whip into a mug. (Insulated mugs keep it colder longer!)
2. Slowly pour your root beer into the mug, and enjoy.

> **TIP:** Freeze your Cool Whip before you go and have the floats on the first day of the trip so it stays as cold as possible.

S'MORE FUN COMBOS

No camping trip is complete without s'mores, so here are a few fun flavor combinations to try!

→ **CLASSIC:** Chocolate + Marshmallow + Graham Cracker

→ **GOOEY:** Chocolate Bar with Caramel Filling + Marshmallow + Graham Cracker

→ **TROPICAL:** White Chocolate + Shredded Coconut + Dried Pineapple Slice + Marshmallow + Graham Cracker

→ **EASTER:** Chocolate + Toasted Peeps + Graham Cracker

→ **FRUITY:** Dark Chocolate + Strawberry Slice + Marshmallow + Graham Cracker

→ **INSTA:** Chocolate Syrup + Marshmallow + Graham Cracker

→ **ELVIS:** Chocolate + Banana + Peanut Butter + Graham Cracker

→ **SPICED:** Chocolate + Cinnamon + Marshmallow + Graham Cracker

→ **OREO:** Chocolate + Marshmallow + Chocolate Sandwich Cookies

→ **SWEET AND SALTY:** Caramel + Marshmallow + Saltine Crackers

PART II

BACKCOUNTRY
CAMPING

Backcountry camping is the perfect way to spend time in nature, see incredible views, and experience the serene tranquility of life on the trail. Obviously, food to fuel that adventure is crucial and often a highlight for weary hikers.

Since everything you take with you in the backcountry needs to be brought in (and out) on your back, careful planning and consideration of weight and space matters. After multiple miles, you'll quickly notice that every ounce counts.

As backpackers spend most of their day getting from one spot to another, it's best to fuel midday with nutrient-dense snacks and count on a hearty breakfast and dinner to start and end the day.

CHAPTER 6

BACKCOUNTRY CAMPING ESSENTIALS

This chapter will cover the basics of backcountry cooking to help you get started in what can sometimes seem to be a very daunting undertaking! In the chapters that follow, I will cover not only what to consider as you plan your backcountry meals, but also how to cook them, and, of course, I'll share my favorite recipes to make.

Backcountry cooking requires an entirely different system than car camping. Things have to be light, efficient, and carefully planned. You don't have the luxury of hauling a stocked kitchen with you, so you need to be sure you have what you need, and only what you need. I'll cover the recommended essentials *and* how to organize them to for the best experience possible.

--- OUTDOOR KITCHEN CHECKLIST ---

The following is a list of must-have items as well as a list of items that are nice to have, but not essential. You'll find as you do more backcountry camping and cooking that you'll quickly tweak this to fit your individual needs. In the meantime, you can get started with the following.

MUST-HAVE KITCHEN ITEMS:

- ☐ 1-liter pot with lid
- ☐ Biodegradable soap
- ☐ Camp mug (ideally with lid and handle)
- ☐ Leakproof oil/sauce storage tubes
- ☐ Lightweight camp stove
- ☐ Matches/lighter/fire starter (have two of the three as backups in case one fails)
- ☐ Pocket knife
- ☐ Pot holders or pot lifter
- ☐ Spork
- ☐ Water filtration system

NICE-TO-HAVE KITCHEN ITEMS:

- ☐ Bear-proof food storage container
- ☐ Chef's knife
- ☐ Foldable spatula/ladle
- ☐ Headlamp or portable lights
- ☐ Lightweight plate/bowl
- ☐ Multi-use towel

--- PANTRY STAPLES ---

Your backcountry pantry should be very simple since you only want to bring what you are going to use. But having some basics on hand at home makes spur-of-the-moment trips that much easier.

- ☐ Bouillon cubes
- ☐ Dried pasta
- ☐ Milk powder
- ☐ Olive oil
- ☐ Peanut butter powder

- ☐ Powdered eggs
- ☐ Salt and black pepper
- ☐ Smoked salmon
- ☐ Sun-dried tomatoes
- ☐ Tuna packets

--- ORGANIZING YOUR BACKCOUNTRY KITCHEN ---

Your backcountry kitchen setup should be fairly simple compared to car camping. There are fewer tools, (hopefully) less mess, and the idea is to use the bare minimum to create delicious meals.

The best tip I have for backcountry cooking in particular is to be organized and do most of your prep work at home. Although this advice is certainly helpful for car camping, too, it's crucial in the backcountry.

HOW TO DEHYDRATE YOUR OWN FOOD

Since every ounce counts in the backcountry, you certainly don't want to be hauling heavy food for miles and days. Food also needs to be mostly shelf stable so it doesn't spoil partway through your trip. Because of this, dehydrated ingredients are super popular among backcountry campers.

You'll notice that many of these recipes contain ingredients that are either purchased already dehydrated or the dehydrating happens in the prep steps. Dehydrating can be a bit intimidating when you're first starting out, but it's an easy process to learn and fun to experiment with.

A dedicated dehydrator is convenient, but you can certainly use the oven you already have to dehydrate full meals for backpacking.

To dehydrate fruit or vegetables, carefully cut them into ¼-inch slices and arrange on a baking sheet lined with parchment paper. Bake at the lowest setting on your oven (below 200°F) for 6 to 8 hours or until dry.

Meat and full meals can also be dehydrated. The trick is getting them very dry without cooking them, which is why the low temperature is needed. Choose lean meats with a low fat content; fatty meats don't dehydrate well and can go rancid.

I like to dehydrate the food I know my family will need on the trail within a couple weeks of camping, and then store them in the fridge or freezer before we leave.

Before you leave home for your trip, lay out every meal you plan to cook, including the utensils you will need to prepare it. Every single thing you will be eating over the course of your backpacking trip needs to be accounted for, including snacks. I always stash a couple of extra granola bars in a hard-to-reach pocket just for emergencies.

I also recommend packing things so that your stove and necessary utensils are easily accessible along with the food for each meal.

→ Food should be packed in reverse order so the items you will need soonest are at the top.
→ Utensils are best stored together in a lightweight mesh bag.

When cooking at camp, pull out everything you will need, get your water boiling right away (for cooking *and* cleaning) and then start prepping your food for that meal.

DAY HIKES

Spending the day hiking is one of my very favorite summer (and spring and fall) activities, and I spend a lot of time with my family on the trail. I also spend a ridiculous amount of time prepping the snacks to fuel those miles. For my family, we have meals that we *only* eat while hiking. Those special dishes are crucial and one of the key factors in keeping my entire family going down the trail.

Happy hikers always have plenty of food in their pack, which usually means taking much more than you expect you'll need. On day hikes you have the perk of only needing to haul the necessities for that day, so you can oftentimes afford to carry the extra weight of a *little* extra food just in case.

Just like backpacking, for longer day hikes it's best to have food that does well even if it gets smashed (because, believe me, it will happen) and that won't spoil quickly. In terms of potential spoilage, a good trick is to add ice to your water bottle and packing your day pack so that the food is placed next to the bottle, keeping it cold. Some of the recipes in this book are perfect for day hiking, too, especially the snacks. However, sometimes you just need to throw something together quickly before you hit the trail. The combinations on page 141 will take you beyond your regular go-tos and give you something to look forward to as the miles go on. You'll notice our sandwich recommendations have strategic ingredient placement to cut down on the possibility of the dreaded soggy bread. I always pack sandwiches in a sealable bag to keep them protected from any potential moisture from a cold water bottle.

The USDA says that perishable foods (like meat and dairy) can go without refrigeration for two hours. You can make the most of that time by using ice packs or, as previously mentioned, packing your food around ice-filled water bottles.

FAMILY-APPROVED TRAIL SANDWICHES INCLUDE:

→ Hot dog bun bottom + PB + banana slices + PB + hot dog bun top

→ Pita pocket + lettuce on both sides + hummus + sliced cucumbers + thin carrot sticks + crumbled feta + olives

→ Dinner roll bottom + goat cheese + prosciutto + arugula + dinner roll top

→ Bagel bottom + smoked Gouda cheese + sliced turkey + Granny Smith apple slices + smoked Gouda cheese + bagel top

→ Focaccia bread bottom + pesto + mozzarella cheese slice + sliced tomato + spinach + mozzarella cheese slice + pesto + focaccia bread top

STOP THE "HANGRY-HIKER" WITH THESE QUICK FIX SNACKS:

→ Chocolate hazelnut pouch + banana chips

→ Cheese stick + salami stick + crackers

→ Pretzels + peanut butter + cinnamon + raisins

→ Dried mango + dried coconut + dried cranberries + cashews

→ Hard-boiled egg + salt and pepper

--- BACKCOUNTRY COOKING ---

When you head into the backcountry, you are heading into a fragile yet awe-inspiring ecosystem. Your job is to enjoy it, not destroy it.

The leave-no-trace principles (page xvi) are especially important for the safety *and* respect of the land and future campers.

Despite the additional factors that go into cooking in the backcountry, many backpackers will say that the food they have on the trail is a highlight of the trip.

Backcountry cooking is more limited not only because of space and weight restrictions, but because many locations prohibit a campfire. This rule is due to the high impact that fires have on the land and for safety reasons. Be sure to research the specific guidelines and regulations for your area before you go, and to abide by them.

One-pan meals that can be cooked over a lightweight stove are ideal and make up most of the recipes in this section.

Simple meals also make it easier to keep a clean camp and discourage wildlife (both large and small) from crashing your camping party. The recipes in this section are particularly formulated to be light to carry, easy to cook, delicious to eat, and full of the energy you need to stay fueled.

CHAPTER 7

BACKCOUNTRY BREAKFAST

Breakfast in the backcountry is so important because it should provide the necessary energy you'll need for pounding out miles on the trail. Like the recipes for car camping breakfasts in chapter 2, some meals in this chapter are quick and simple so you can get going early, and some take a little longer, giving you permission to just enjoy the morning.

PECAN RAISIN GRANOLA

GLUTEN-FREE, VEGETARIAN

SERVES 5 / PREP TIME: 10 MINUTES / COOK TIME: 45 MINUTES

This is a good recipe to make ahead of time and bring for breakfast on the trail. It provides great energy, travels well, and can be used as a snack, too. We eat it on its own or over yogurt on the first couple days of the trail. It's best to use a baking sheet with a lip on the perimeter to contain the granola during baking.

½ cup dark brown sugar

¼ cup pure maple syrup

½ cup vegetable oil

½ teaspoon salt

3 cups rolled oats

2 teaspoons ground cinnamon

1 cup pecans, roughly chopped

½ cup pumpkin seeds

1 cup golden raisins

1. Preheat the oven to 325°F and line a large baking sheet with parchment paper.

2. In a saucepan, combine the brown sugar, maple syrup, vegetable oil, and salt. Cook over low heat, stirring frequently, until the mixture is hot and bubbly. Remove from heat and set aside.

3. In a large bowl, combine the oats, cinnamon, pecans, and pumpkin seeds. Pour the dry ingredients into the sugar mixture and stir to coat evenly.

4. Spread the entire mixture onto the lined baking sheet and bake until golden brown, about 40 minutes, stirring every 10 minutes. You want it golden, but not overbaked.

5. After about 40 minutes, remove the baking sheet from the oven and carefully stir in the raisins. Cook for about 5 more minutes, then remove from oven and let cool.

6. Break into chunks and pack into resealable plastic bags.

ALPINE SCRAMBLE

GLUTEN-FREE

SERVES 2 / PREP TIME: 15 MINUTES / COOK TIME: 15 MINUTES

A hearty breakfast is the best way to start the morning for sustainable energy all day, no matter what activities you have planned. It takes a bit of time to dehydrate the veggies, but it's worth it. This recipe brings together protein-packed eggs and hearty veggies in a lightweight, easy-to-pack dish.

2 tablespoons onion, chopped

1 cup chopped zucchini

½ cup sliced mushrooms

1 cup spinach

6 tablespoons dried egg powder

1 tablespoon garlic powder

¼ teaspoon salt

Dash black pepper

1 cup warm water plus ¾ cup, divided

2 tablespoons olive oil

2 tablespoons Parmesan cheese

PREP AT HOME

1. Lay the onion, zucchini, mushrooms, and spinach out separately on baking sheets and dehydrate at 135°F for 6 to 8 hours or until dry.

2. Pack the dried spinach, egg powder, garlic powder, salt, and pepper in a resealable plastic bag.

3. In a second bag, pack the dehydrated mushrooms and zucchini.

4. Add 1 cup of warm water to the mushroom and zucchini bag to rehydrate. When the desired texture is reached (around 15 minutes), carefully drain off the excess water.

5. Heat the olive oil in a skillet.

6. Add ¾ cup of water to the egg powder, spinach, and spice bag. Mix well.

7. Dump the egg mixture into the pan along with the mushrooms and zucchini and cook until the desired doneness, stirring frequently.

8. Top with Parmesan cheese and eat warm.

> **TIP:** If you prefer meat with your eggs, just add a few tablespoons of bacon bits.

EASY EGG SANDWICH

NUT-FREE

SERVES 2 / PREP TIME: 5 MINUTES / COOK TIME: 10 MINUTES

Croissants travel surprisingly well in the backcountry and add a little extra taste of awesome to an open-air breakfast. My family reserves these sandwiches for backpacking only, which makes them even more of a treat. It's also difficult to eat just one of these croissants, so feel free to double the recipe!

2 croissants, halved lengthwise

½ cup freeze-dried eggs

1 tablespoon bacon bits

½ teaspoon black pepper

2 slices pepper Jack cheese

¾ cup water

1 teaspoon olive oil

1 whole unripe avocado

PREP AT HOME

1. Wrap the halved croissants in a paper towel, then in a plastic resealable plastic bag.

2. Pack the eggs, bacon bits, and pepper together in another resealable plastic bag. Write "add ¾ cup of water" on the baggie.

3. Pack cheese slices in another small resealable plastic bag.

4. Refrigerate the eggs and bacon and the cheese until ready to use, then transfer to a cooler for transporting to the campsite.

5. Add the water to the powdered eggs and mix well while still in the bag.

6. Heat the olive oil in a frying pan over a camp stove. Add the contents of egg and bacon baggie and scramble until cooked completely.

7. Divide the eggs, cheese slices, and avocado between the two croissants. You can carefully grill them on your already hot frying pan to melt the cheese if desired, then serve.

> **TIP:** When choosing an avocado, you definitely don't want a squishy one that will spoil quickly in your pack. Choose one that is still firm, and it will be perfect 2 to 3 days later when you're ready for it.

WHILE-YOU-SLEEP OATS

DAIRY-FREE, GLUTEN-FREE, VEGETARIAN

SERVES 2 / PREP TIME: 5 MINUTES, PLUS OVERNIGHT TO SET

This is a super easy no-cook option for backpacking so you can spend less time cooking breakfast and get on the trail quicker. If you don't mind the extra weight, you can always make it with shelf-stable almond milk instead of water. Either works great and they both taste delicious.

1 cup rolled oats

2 teaspoons ground cinnamon

⅓ cup dried cranberries

Pinch salt

1 cup water

½ cup chopped walnuts

PREP AT HOME

1. Combine the rolled oats, cinnamon, cranberries, and salt in a medium-size resealable plastic bag.

AT THE CAMPSITE

2. The night before you would like to eat this for breakfast, add the water to the resealable plastic bag. Gently squeeze to combine. Store in a safe place overnight.

3. In the morning, add the walnuts and enjoy!

BAGEL WITH SMOKED SALMON

NUT-FREE

SERVES 6 / **PREP TIME:** 5 MINUTES

This breakfast is so simple but seems like such a treat in the backcountry. Bagels travel well when sealed in bags, and individual cream cheese packets can last up to 2 weeks without refrigeration. Although this recipe technically feeds 6, we usually wrap up extra bagels and eat them for lunch or even as a snack.

1 (6-count) package
onion bagels

6 individual cream
cheese packets

6 ounces smoked salmon

1. If desired, split and toast the bagels on a campfire or over a camp stove.
2. Spread 1 packet of cream cheese on each bagel.
3. Lay about an ounce of smoked salmon on top of each bagel, and serve.

> **TIP:** You can use any flavor of bagels for this recipe. Besides onion, I love it with everything bagels, plain bagels, and whole-wheat bagels.

BLUEBERRY CORNMEAL PANCAKES

DAIRY-FREE, NUT-FREE, VEGAN

SERVES 3 TO 4 / **PREP TIME:** 5 MINUTES / **COOK TIME:** 20 MINUTES

I love the texture of these cornmeal pancakes. If you happen to not usually be a fan of pancakes, I bet these will be just enough different to renew your faith in this classic breakfast. When they're made small, like silver dollar–size pancakes, they are easy to transport and even easier to snack on.

¾ cup cornmeal

¾ cup whole-wheat flour

½ cup dried blueberries

½ cup raw wheat germ

½ cup milk powder

2 teaspoons baking powder

½ teaspoon salt

1½ cups water

2 tablespoons canola oil

Maple syrup, for topping (optional)

PREP AT HOME

1. Combine the cornmeal, whole-wheat flour, blueberries, wheat germ, milk powder, baking powder, and salt in a gallon-size resealable plastic bag, and seal.

AT THE CAMPSITE

2. Add the water to the resealable plastic bag. Seal and massage to mix.
3. Heat the oil on a skillet over medium-high heat.
4. Pour the batter directly from the bag in small circles (about 3 inches in diameter).

5. Cook until air bubbles form at the edges of the pancakes. Flip and cook for an additional 2 to 3 minutes or until both sides are golden brown.
6. Serve with maple syrup (if using).

TIP: I recommend writing on your plastic bag "add 1½ cups of water" so you remember when you get to the campsite. These pancakes also make great snacks for the trail, so try doubling the recipe.

CHOCOLATE PEANUT BUTTER OATMEAL

DAIRY-FREE, VEGAN

SERVES 1 / PREP TIME: 5 MINUTES / COOK TIME: 5 MINUTES

Love chocolate and peanut butter together? Yeah, me too. Sometimes we all just need a little chocolate fix to get the day going. This is a great meal to make right in your insulated mug, so it's a "serves 1" recipe, but feel free to double or triple it and make it in a large pot if cooking for a crowd.

½ cup instant oats

1 teaspoon cocoa powder

1 teaspoon chia seeds

¼ cup freeze-dried banana slices

1 teaspoon ground cinnamon (optional)

1 travel-size packet peanut butter

1 cup boiling water

PREP AT HOME

1. Put the oats, cocoa powder, chia seeds, banana slices, and cinnamon (if using) in a small resealable plastic bag.
2. Add the peanut butter to the bag, too, but keep it unopened in its packet.

AT THE CAMPSITE

3. Remove the peanut butter packet from the bag and dump the rest of the contents into your insulated mug.

4. Slowly add the boiling water, and stir until the desired consistency.
5. Open the peanut butter packet and stir into the oatmeal.

TIP: I love peanut butter, but this oatmeal also tastes great with cashew or almond butter if you prefer those or have a peanut allergy.

BACKCOUNTRY CHIA PUDDING

DAIRY-FREE, VEGETARIAN

SERVES 4 / PREP TIME: 20 MINUTES

Chia seeds are a fantastic superfood with many benefits. They are high in fiber, protein, and omega-3 fatty acids, all of which are great for sustainable energy on the trail. I personally love the consistency of this pudding, and that little bit of honey makes it taste like dessert.

1 cup chia seeds, divided

4 (8-ounce) individual vanilla almond milk cartons

1 cup dried blueberries

¼ cup honey (optional)

Nuts, for topping (optional)

1. Add ¼ cup of chia seeds each in 4 separate resealable plastic bags.
2. Pour an entire carton of almond milk into each of the bags.
3. Add the blueberries and honey (if using).
4. Let soak for 20 to 30 minutes.
5. Top with nuts (if using) and enjoy!

CHAPTER 8

BACKCOUNTRY DINNERS

I like to make these backcountry dinners not only to save money, but also so I can take some of my family's favorite meals out on the trail. This chapter includes some recipes that you will dehydrate on your own (in your oven or in a dehydrator), and many others that don't require any special methods or ingredients, providing flexibility to your trip. I find it beneficial to do a "dry backpacking run" at home to test out which meals my family will love so I know what to bring with us.

CONTINUED>

CONTINUED

BEEF JERKY STEW

DAIRY-FREE, GLUTEN-FREE, NUT-FREE

SERVES 2 TO 4 / PREP TIME: 5 MINUTES / COOK TIME: 1 HOUR

Beef jerky is such a staple while backpacking. It's excellent on its own, and it easily enhances a comforting dinner of stew on the trail.

1 cup dried tomato

1 cup beef jerky
(½-inch chunks)

1 cup dried potato chunks

1 tablespoon dried
bell pepper

1 tablespoon dried
onion flakes

½ teaspoon dried basil

½ teaspoon dried oregano

½ teaspoon dried
garlic flakes

Salt and black pepper

3 cups water

2 carrots, sliced (optional)

PREP AT HOME

1. Combine the tomato, beef jerky, potatoes, bell pepper, onion, basil, oregano, garlic, and salt and black pepper to taste in a large resealable plastic bag.

AT THE CAMPSITE

2. Add the resealable plastic bag of dried foods to the water in a saucepan, and let sit for 30 minutes to rehydrate.

3. After 30 minutes, place the pan over medium heat and bring to a boil.

4. Add sliced fresh carrot (if using) and simmer until the jerky is tender, 30 minutes to 1 hour.

SHEPHERD'S PIE BOWL

NUT-FREE

SERVES 2 / PREP TIME: 5 MINUTES / COOK TIME: 20 MINUTES

I love shepherd's pie at home, and this simple portable version is always a hit in the backcountry, too. This recipe uses a variety of dried ingredients to cut down on weight, but the flavor remains the same.

½ cup freeze-dried veggie medley (peas, corn, carrots)

⅓ cup chopped dried mushrooms

¼ teaspoon dried rosemary

½ teaspoon dried thyme

1 (8-ounce) packet brown gravy

2 ounces instant mashed potatoes

3 tablespoons butter

Pinch black pepper

3½ cups water

1 (5-ounce) can ham

PREP AT HOME

1. Divide the veggies, mushrooms, rosemary, thyme, and gravy between two sealable bags.

2. Put the instant mashed potatoes, butter, and pepper in a third sealable bag.

3. Write "add 1 cup of water" on each of the three bags to easily remember at camp.

AT THE CAMPSITE

4. Bring the water to a boil.

5. Divide the ham between the two bags of veggies.

6. Add 1 cup of hot water to each of the three bags. Stir well and loosely close (but don't seal).

7. After 5 minutes, scoop out a large spoonful of the potato mixture into each of the veggie bags and mix well to thicken.

8. Top with the remaining potatoes, and eat right out of the bag.

TIP: Resealable plastic freezer bags are preferred for all recipes, but particularly this one. The bag will be very hot when you add the water, so let it sit to cool for a few minutes somewhere other than your lap.

SWEET POTATO, CHORIZO, AND BLACK BEAN SKILLET

DAIRY-FREE, GLUTEN-FREE, NUT-FREE

SERVES 4 / **PREP TIME:** 25 MINUTES, PLUS 6 TO 8 HOURS TO DEHYDRATE /
COOK TIME: 15 MINUTES

This recipe is one I make entirely at home, dehydrate in the oven, and then reconstitute on the trail. It's even better to make a double batch at home, eat some, and then dehydrate the rest for a backpacking dinner.

½ tablespoon olive oil

1 small sweet potato, peeled and chopped into ½-inch cubes

½ sweet onion, chopped

6 ounces Mexican-style pork chorizo

½ cup black beans

1¾ cups chicken broth

1 cup corn

1 (4-ounce) can diced green chiles

½ cup long-grain white rice

Chopped cilantro (optional)

PREP AT HOME

1. Heat the olive oil in a large, ovenproof skillet on medium heat. Add the sweet potato and onion and sauté for 5 minutes or until just tender.

2. Add the chorizo and sauté until cooked through, breaking it up as it cooks.

3. Add the black beans, chicken broth, corn, and green chiles to the skillet and bring to a boil over high heat.

4. Add the rice and stir to combine. Turn the heat to low, cover, and simmer until the rice is tender, about 18 minutes. Add extra chicken broth if needed.

5. While the rice is cooking, preheat the oven to 135°F.
6. After rice has cooked, spread the entire mixture out onto a baking sheet. Place the sheet in the oven and dehydrate for 6 to 8 hours, or until fully dry.
7. Once cool, transfer the mixture to a large resealable plastic bag.

AT THE CAMPSITE
8. In a pot, combine equal parts water and the dehydrated meal and let sit for 5 minutes to soak.
9. Bring to a boil, turn the heat to low, and simmer for 5 to 7 minutes.
10. Turn off the heat and let sit for about 10 minutes until completely rehydrated. Stir, top with cilantro (if using), and enjoy.

BACKCOUNTRY EASY POCKET PIZZA

NUT-FREE

SERVES 4 / PREP TIME: 5 MINUTES / COOK TIME: 15 MINUTES

Yes, you can even have pizza while backpacking! This pizza is a real treat to have a couple of days into the trip and features ingredients that pack well on the trail. I like to fold mine over so I can heat both sides on our backcountry stove. If, however, you know you'll be able to have a fire, you can also warm it on some tinfoil.

1 (4.5-ounce) tube tomato paste

4 pieces naan or pita bread

6 mozzarella string cheeses (or 1 cup shredded cheese if desired)

1 tablespoon pizza seasoning

Pepperoni (optional)

Diced pineapple (optional)

1. Divide the tomato paste evenly among each piece of naan or pita bread.

2. Top with the mozzarella cheese, pepperoni (if using), pineapple (if using), and pizza seasoning. If using cheese sticks, split them up so they cover the bread.

3. Fold the bread in half and warm in tinfoil over a fire or grill on your camp stove until the cheese has melted.

TIP: To make your own pizza seasoning, mix equal parts onion powder, garlic powder, and oregano.

WILDERNESS CHARCUTERIE BOARD

SERVES 4 / **PREP TIME:** 10 MINUTES

This recipe is the ultimate "appetizer" while backpacking and totally works as a full meal, too. The best part is it is totally customizable and can be made nut-free, vegetarian, or gluten-free. The key is variety and sticking with ingredients that have a long shelf life. Below is a variety of options with instructions for amounts I recommend for two people sharing.

OPTIONAL INGREDIENTS

Jerky

Salami

Cheddar cheese

Crackers

Pretzels

Trail mix

Smoked fish

Mixed nuts

Dried fruit

Dehydrated hummus

PREP AT HOME

1. Choose 2 to 3 meats and 2 to 3 cheeses and slice them to your preference.
2. Pack 2 different nuts, 2 different dried fruits, and 2 or 3 different grains each in their own plastic bags.
3. Pack up the dehydrated hummus (if using).

AT THE CAMPSITE

4. Lay out the different options on a clean surface.
5. Mix the hummus with water (if using). Enjoy!

TRAIL JAMBALAYA

NUT-FREE, GLUTEN-FREE

SERVES 2 / **PREP TIME:** 5 MINUTES / **COOK TIME:** 25 MINUTES

This one-pot meal is packed full of flavor, which is always welcome after a long day on the trail. I like to include smoked sausages for extra protein and flavor, but you certainly could leave them out.

1 precooked andouille sausage link or smoked sausage

½ cup dehydrated black beans

½ cup mixed dehydrated veggies (tomatoes, peppers, and celery, for example)

1 tablespoon dried onion flakes

2 teaspoons dried garlic flakes

1 cup quick cooking rice

1½ cups water

1 chicken bouillon cube

¼ cup ketchup

1 (7-ounce) package precooked shredded chicken

Creole seasoning

PREP AT HOME

1. Slice the andouille sausage and freeze in a resealable plastic bag until you're ready to leave.
2. Pack the dried beans, dried veggies, dried onion flakes, and dried garlic flakes in a separate resealable plastic bag.

AT THE CAMPSITE

3. In a large pot, bring the rice, water, bouillon cube, and ketchup to a boil and cook for 1 minute. Remove from heat. The mixture should be slightly runny.

4. Add the dried beans, dried veggies, dried onion flakes, and dried garlic flakes to the pot. Add the sausage and chicken. Add the creole seasoning to taste.
5. Add water as needed to rehydrate, a little at a time.
6. Cook for 5 more minutes to let the flavors blend, stirring constantly. Serve warm.

TIP: When using sausage, I recommend eating this sooner than later on your trip just to save on weight. However, for longer trips, shelf-stable salami or even jerky works, too. There is just something very satisfying about having some full-fat sausage on the trail after a long day that makes it worth carrying the weight. Since the sausage is frozen before you go, it can last longer on the trail.

CHEESY BACON AND ONION MASHERS

GLUTEN-FREE, NUT-FREE

SERVES 1 / **PREP TIME:** 5 MINUTES / **COOK TIME:** 8 MINUTES

This recipe serves just one because it's easier to prepare in an insulated mug for easy eating. Of course, you can multiply it as needed and make it in a large pot. If you have a larger crowd, double or triple this recipe. Prepare the ingredients as directed, then when you're ready to eat, bring the water to a boil, remove from heat, then add all the ingredients to the pot and stir well. Let cool, then serve to your hungry crowd.

¾ cup instant mashed potatoes

2 tablespoons dried milk

1 tablespoon dried onion

¼ teaspoon black pepper

1 ounce French onion shelf-stable cheese (such as Laughing Cow)

3 tablespoons shelf-stable bacon

1¼ cups boiling water

PREP AT HOME

1. Pack the instant mashed potatoes, dried milk, dried onion, and pepper in a sealable bag.
2. Pack the bacon in a separate sealable bag.

AT THE CAMPSITE

3. Unwrap the cheese and place it in the bottom of your mug. Add the bacon and dried ingredients.
4. Pour in the boiling water and stir well.
5. Cover tightly and let sit for 5 minutes, or until cool enough to eat.

PUMPKIN CURRY WITH SPINACH AND CHICKPEAS

GLUTEN-FREE, VEGAN

SERVES 2 / **PREP TIME:** 5 MINUTES / **COOK TIME:** 8 MINUTES

The combination of pumpkin and curry flavors is warm and inviting for cool evenings on the trail. I love the creamy texture in this recipe in particular. Love a little spice? Kick up the heat by adding a little more curry!

½ cup dehydrated cooked basmati rice

½ cup dehydrated canned chickpeas

3 cups dehydrated spinach

¼ cup pumpkin powder

1 tablespoon mild curry powder

¼ cup coconut milk powder

1 cup water

Pinch salt

PREP AT HOME

1. Mix all the ingredients except for the water and salt in a sealable bag.

AT THE CAMPSITE

2. Pour the dry curry mixture into a pot. Add the water and stir well.
3. Bring to a boil over medium heat.
4. Cook, stirring occasionally, for 10 minutes. Let stand for 5 minutes to cool.
5. Season with salt to taste.

> **TIP:** Pumpkin powder can be found at natural grocery stores or online. It adds a great deal of flavor and nutrients to vegetarian dishes.

VEGAN TORTILLA SOUP

DAIRY-FREE, GLUTEN-FREE, NUT-FREE, VEGAN

SERVES 2 / **PREP TIME:** 10 MINUTES, PLUS 8 HOURS TO DEHYDRATE /
COOK TIME: 15 MINUTES

This soup recipe starts with dehydrating all the ingredients at home first (in a dehydrator or oven) and finishes by rehydrating on the trail. It's packed full of flavor and is a satisfying, hearty meal. It's also fantastic cold!

1 small onion

1 (15-ounce) can black beans

1 (4-ounce) can mild green chiles

1 (15 ounce) can fire-roasted tomatoes

1 cup frozen roasted corn

2 tablespoons fresh cilantro

2 vegetable bouillon cubes

½ teaspoon chili powder

½ teaspoon garlic powder

½ teaspoon cumin

2½ cups water

2 cups tortilla chips

PREP AT HOME

1. Chop the onion. Drain and rinse the black beans and green chiles.

2. Place the onion, black beans, green chiles, tomatoes, roasted corn, and cilantro on a baking sheet and bake in the oven set as low as it can go (about 135 to 200°F) for 8 hours, or until every-thing is dry.

3. Once dry, let cool for several minutes, then place the dried veggies into a resealable plastic bag and add the bouillon cubes, chili powder, garlic powder, and cumin, and seal.

AT THE CAMPSITE

4. Once at camp, add the bag of dried ingredients to the water and simmer until rehydrated. Add more water as needed.

5. Top with crushed tortilla chips and enjoy!

> **TIP:** I recommend writing on your resealable plastic bag "start with 2½ cups of water" so you remember how much you need to add at camp.

FREEZER-BAG CHICKEN, VEGGIES, AND RICE

DAIRY-FREE, GLUTEN-FREE, NUT-FREE

SERVES 2 / PREP TIME: 5 MINUTES / COOK TIME: 10 MINUTES

This recipe is super simple, but can be dressed up with your favorite seasonings if desired. My kids like it as listed below, but sometimes we adults add a little Tabasco sauce to give it a kick.

2 cups instant white rice

⅓ cup vegetable soup mix

⅓ cup freeze-dried chicken

2 tablespoons freeze-dried celery

⅓ cup freeze-dried mixed veggies

2 teaspoons garlic powder

2 tablespoons olive oil

¼ teaspoon salt

¼ teaspoon black pepper

2½ cups water

PREP AT HOME

1. Combine all the ingredients except for the water in a large resealable plastic freezer bag.

AT THE CAMPSITE

2. Boil the water. Add the water to the resealable plastic bag with the dried ingredients and let sit for 5 minutes. Stir and enjoy!

BACKCOUNTRY TUNA CASSEROLE

NUT-FREE

SERVES 2 / **PREP TIME:** 10 MINUTES / **COOK TIME:** 15 MINUTES

This casserole is hands-down my family's favorite backcountry meal. The tuna gives it a huge punch of protein and it's easy to cook right at camp. Don't leave out the fried onions—the added texture makes all the difference.

1 box organic mac and cheese, noodles and cheese powder divided

½ cup freeze-dried peas

¼ teaspoon garlic powder

½ teaspoon onion powder

¼ teaspoon black pepper

½ cup crispy fried onions

¼ cup Parmesan cheese

1¼ cups water

1 (6-ounce) pouch tuna

PREP AT HOME

1. Place the mac and cheese noodles, cheese packet, dried peas, garlic powder, onion powder, and pepper in a resealable bag. Mix well.
2. In a separate bag, add the fried onions and Parmesan cheese.

AT THE CAMPSITE

3. Simmer the contents of the noodle bag and the water in a pot until the noodles and peas are tender, 9 to 10 minutes.
4. Add the tuna, fried onions and Parmesan cheese, and mix well. Enjoy warm.

VEGETARIAN TORTELLINI

VEGETARIAN

SERVES 2 TO 3 / PREP TIME: 10 MINUTES / COOK TIME: 15 MINUTES

Tortellini is a favorite dish in my family and definitely a treat on the trail. It packs a lot of flavor and is a filling meal, yet it's one of the easiest and lightest meals to make. You can also dress this up with any extra dehydrated veggies you would like to haul (spinach, squash, etc.).

10 ounces dried tortellini

2 ounces sun-dried tomatoes

2 ounces pesto

¼ cup olive oil

3 cups water

2 ounces pine nuts

2 tablespoons Parmesan cheese

PREP AT HOME

1. Combine the tortellini and sun-dried tomatoes in a resealable plastic bag. Make a note on the bag for how long to cook the tortellini (see the package directions).

2. Put the pesto and olive oil in a separate resealable plastic bag together.

3. Pack the pine nuts and Parmesan cheese in a separate resealable plastic bag together.

4. Refrigerate the pesto and the pine nut bag until ready to use, then transfer to a cooler for transporting to the campsite.

5. Bring the water to a boil. Add the pasta and tomatoes and cook according to the package directions you wrote on the bag.

6. Drain the pasta carefully using the lid from your pot.

7. Add the pesto and olive oil and stir well. Garnish with the pine nuts and Parmesan and serve warm.

YELLOW CURRY WITH RICE

DAIRY-FREE, NUT-FREE, VEGAN

**SERVES 2 / PREP TIME: 10 MINUTES, PLUS 6 HOURS TO DEHYDRATE /
COOK TIME: 15 MINUTES**

I love curry and while it's very easy to make, it seems like such a treat on the
trail. If you want to add meat to this vegetarian dish, I suggest bringing a pack of
shredded chicken and adding it in at the end.

½ cup basmati rice

2 cups frozen mixed
stir-fry veggies

1 teaspoon curry powder

¼ cup coconut milk powder

2 cups water

Salt and black pepper

PREP AT HOME

1. Cook the rice according to the package directions. Drain and cool.

2. Spread the cooked rice and vegetables on trays
   lined with parchment paper.

3. Dry in an oven or dehydrator at 135°F for about
   6 hours or until dry.

4. Pack the dried rice and dried vegetables together
   in a large resealable plastic bag. Add the curry
   powder and coconut milk powder and seal.

5. Combine the rice, curry, and vegetable mix with the water in your cooking pot.
6. Bring to a boil over medium heat.
7. Cook for about 5 minutes, stirring occasionally.
8. Remove from heat, cover, and let stand 10 minutes to finish rehydrating.
9. Add salt and pepper to taste.

TIP: Not a huge fan of stir-fry veggies? This recipe works fine with any vegetables you prefer. Some options include a traditional mix of corn, peas, and carrots, or red and green bell peppers.

PESTO GNOCCHI WITH SUN-DRIED TOMATOES

SERVES 2 / COOK TIME: 15 MINUTES

This meal isn't entirely lightweight, but sometimes a meal that doesn't just consist of rehydrated foods is worth the little extra effort to haul it in. I recommend you plan this for one of the first days of your backpacking trip and enjoy a pile of flavor packed in an easy-to-cook meal.

1 pound gnocchi

4 tablespoons pesto paste

2 ounces sun-dried tomatoes

2 tablespoons Parmesan cheese (optional)

1. Bring a medium pot of water to a boil. Add the gnocchi and sun-dried tomatoes and cook for 2 to 3 minutes.

2. Drain the gnocchi. Stir in the pesto. Top with Parmesan cheese if desired.

> **TIP:** I recommend using pesto paste opposed to dried pesto packets just for better flavor and ease of carrying. Since you only need a little bit of Parmesan cheese, you can just add a couple packets from a convenience store, or alternatively, pack the small amount in a resealable plastic bag to bring with you.

CHAPTER 9

BACKCOUNTRY SNACKS

Even more so than car camping snacks, backcountry snacks are 100 percent necessary to do right. They ward off some nasty cases of hangry hikers, keep morale up as the miles tick by, and provide something to look forward to when the going is rough. I encourage you to take the time to prep these snacks before you go, make double batches if you wish, and then have them ready for backpacking and hiking all summer long.

ROASTED SPICED ALMONDS

VEGETARIAN

SERVES 6 / PREP TIME: 10 MINUTES / COOK TIME: 20 MINUTES

Almonds are a great source of healthy fats, fiber, magnesium, protein, and vitamin E. Since they're prepped at home, I love that they are an easy snack to transport as you hike, and even easier to pop a few for quick energy. These savory spiced almonds are full of flavor, and a favorite recipe for the trail.

2 tablespoons melted butter

2 teaspoons Worcestershire sauce

1½ teaspoons chili powder

½ teaspoon cumin

½ teaspoon garlic powder

½ teaspoon dried basil

¼ teaspoon onion powder

½ teaspoon cayenne pepper

1½ cups whole raw almonds

½ teaspoon sea salt

1. Preheat the oven to 350°F and line a baking sheet with parchment paper.

2. In a large bowl, whisk together the butter, Worcestershire sauce, chili powder, cumin, garlic powder, basil, onion powder, and cayenne pepper. Add the almonds and toss to coat.

3. Spread the almonds in a single layer on the lined baking sheet and bake for 18 to 20 minutes, flipping every few minutes.

4. Remove from oven and sprinkle with sea salt.

5. Let cool completely before packing in a sealable bag.

POWER TRAIL BITES

GLUTEN-FREE, VEGETARIAN

SERVES 2 TO 4 / PREP TIME: 5 MINUTES, PLUS 2 HOURS TO CHILL

Here's a little secret: I totally hike for chocolate. These Power Trail Bites not only provide some great protein, but they also contain chocolate chips, which makes all the difference. These are a huge hit for hikers (and non-hikers) of all ages.

1 cup quick oats

½ cup unsweetened shredded coconut

¼ cup sunflower seeds

¼ cup raisins

¼ cup chopped walnuts

¼ cup chopped peanuts

¼ cup mini chocolate chips or vegan chocolate chips

¾ cup natural peanut butter

¼ cup maple syrup

1. Dump all the ingredients into a large bowl.
2. Mix with your hands to blend everything together.
3. Form the mixture into balls, using about 2 tablespoons of dough per ball. Place the formed balls on a baking sheet or plate.
4. Let chill and harden in the fridge for about 2 hours. Pack in a resealable plastic bag for easy access on the trail.

HOMEMADE STRAWBERRY RHUBARB FRUIT LEATHER

DAIRY-FREE, GLUTEN-FREE, NUT-FREE, VEGAN

SERVES 4 / PREP TIME: 5 MINUTES, PLUS 3 TO 4 HOURS TO DEHYDRATE

Fruit leather is a great trail treat, especially for kids. (Though every honest adult will tell you they love it, too.) Though drying them takes a little time, these snacks are made with just a few healthy ingredients and pack easily. I love saving a little money and knowing exactly what goes into this fruit leather.

The zing of ginger elevates this snack to another level and brings out the flavor of the strawberry and rhubarb. If your kids are picky, you can leave the ginger out.

2 cups strawberries

1 cup rhubarb, chopped

1 tablespoon freshly squeezed lemon juice

3 tablespoons maple syrup

1 tablespoon fresh ginger or 1 teaspoon ginger powder (optional)

1. Wash the strawberries and trim the stems off. Chop the rhubarb.

2. Place the strawberries, rhubarb, lemon juice, maple syrup, and ginger (if using) in a blender or food processor and puree for about a minute until smooth.

3. Preheat the oven to the lowest temperature (most start at about 170°F). Do not go any hotter than 200°F.

4. Line a baking sheet with parchment paper and spread the fruit mixture evenly on the paper. It should be about ⅛ inch thick.
5. Cook in the oven for 3 to 4 hours until the mixture is tacky, but not sticky. Remove from oven.
6. While still warm, carefully peel the leather from the parchment paper and lay on plastic wrap. Wrap the leather and the plastic wrap together and then store in an airtight bag in the refrigerator.
7. Pack in an airtight container or resealable plastic bag for transportation to the trail.

TIP: To cut down on dry time and make it easier to store, drop the mixture on the parchment paper in circles about 4 inches in diameter. Alternatively, you can dry in one large sheet and then cut with a pizza cutter into strips.

HUMMUS AND VEGGIES

DAIRY-FREE, GLUTEN-FREE, VEGAN

SERVES 2 / PREP TIME: 5 MINUTES

Hummus and veggies are a favorite lunch or snack combo at home, and they work equally well on the trail with a little planning and the joy of dehydration. Plain hummus works, but the seasonings in this recipe give it a little extra flavor.

1 cup powdered hummus

2 tablespoons chopped sun-dried tomatoes

Everything bagel seasoning

1 tablespoon olive oil (a single-serve packet is ideal for this)

Dried veggie chips, for serving

1½ cups water

PREP AT HOME

1. Combine the powdered hummus, sun-dried tomatoes, and bagel seasoning in a resealable plastic bag.

2. Pack the veggie chips in another bag.

AT THE CAMPSITE

3. On the trail, add the water and olive oil to the hummus and mix well.

4. Dip chips right into the bag for an easy lunch!

> **TIP:** Not a fan of dried veggie chips? Other dipper options include pretzel rods, any crackers that don't crumble, or fresh veggies (if you will be eating them at the beginning of the trip).

TRAIL GORP

VEGETARIAN

SERVES 6 / PREP TIME: 5 MINUTES

Trail GORP (Good Old Raisins and Peanuts) has been a staple in our family from the very beginning. In fact, it took a centerpiece on all the tables at our wedding. It is the hiking snack to beat all hiking snacks with a perfect blend of sweet and salty that just hits the spot. It's absolutely worth a little weight in your pack. We mix up a big bag and try to stretch it as long as we can (which usually isn't very long).

1 cup chocolate chips

1 cup honey-roasted peanuts

1 cup raisins

1 cup pretzel nuggets

1 cup cashews

1 cup cereal of choice

1. Dump everything in a large resealable plastic bag and shake to combine.

2. Divide into individual resealable plastic bags as needed for the trail.

TIP: Trail GORP is the easiest thing to customize. Just dump anything you want in a big bag and go with it. Hint: You can never have too much chocolate. Feel free to add candy-coated chocolates (like M&Ms) to this mix on top of the chocolate chips, or, if you will be in hot temperatures, replace the chocolate chips with the M&Ms for less melting potential.

SWEET AND SALTY SRIRACHA TRAIL MIX

VEGETARIAN

SERVES 6 / **PREP TIME:** 5 MINUTES / **COOK TIME:** 15 MINUTES

When you're sweating on the trail, salty food not only tastes good, but it's also necessary to replace lost electrolytes. This snack pairs that salt with a little sweet and a little spicy. My kids are always just excited for any excuse to eat Cheddar fish crackers.

2 cups mini pretzels

2 cups Cheddar fish crackers

2 cups square Cheddar cheese crackers

2 cups rice cereal

2 cups oyster crackers

1 cup chopped almonds

1 cup chopped cashews

6 tablespoons butter, melted

¼ cup Worcestershire sauce

¼ cup Sriracha

2 tablespoons honey

1 teaspoon garlic powder

1 teaspoon salt

1. Preheat the oven to 300°F.
2. Combine the pretzels, fish crackers, square crackers, rice cereal, oyster crackers, almonds, and cashews in a large bowl.
3. Combine the butter, Worcestershire sauce, Sriracha, honey, garlic powder, and salt in a medium bowl.
4. Pour the liquid mixture over the dry mixture and stir well to combine, making sure everything is coated.
5. Line a baking sheet with parchment paper and spread the mixture evenly over the paper.

6. Bake at 300°F for 15 minutes or until slightly golden. Check often to prevent burning.
7. Cool completely and then pack in an airtight container or resealable plastic baggie.

TIP: I use my family's favorite blend of crackers in this recipe, but you can use whatever crackers you have in your pantry and it will still taste great. This mix makes 12 cups, so it's plenty for a couple of camping trips or to share with friends. It will last a week in an airtight container.

PEANUT BUTTER AND JELLY BARS

GLUTEN-FREE, VEGETARIAN

MAKES 16 BARS / PREP TIME: 15 MINUTES, PLUS 2 TO 4 HOURS TO CHILL / COOK TIME: 30 MINUTES

Peanut butter and jelly on the trail? It's possible with these bars. I like to make mine with strawberry jam, but feel free to use whatever flavor is to your taste—they work with any fruit jam. These bars are a huge favorite in my home of peanut butter and jelly lovers!

2 cups gluten-free rolled oats

2 cups raw almonds

½ teaspoon salt

¼ cup brown sugar

½ cup plus 2 tablespoons butter

1 cup strawberry jam

½ cup peanut butter

1 cup chopped peanuts

1. Preheat the oven to 350°F. Line a 9-by-13-inch pan with parchment paper.

2. In a food processor or high-speed blender, pulse the oats, almonds, salt, and brown sugar into a fine meal.

3. Melt ½ cup of butter. Transfer the almond oat mixture to a bowl and add the butter. Mix until well combined.

4. Press the mixture into the bottom of the pan in an even layer. I suggest getting your hands wet with cold water and pressing hard with your fingers for best results.

5. Bake the crust for 15 minutes.
6. Meanwhile, heat the jam, peanut butter, and the remaining 2 tablespoons of butter in a small saucepan. Bring to a boil and simmer for about 5 minutes until slightly thickened.
7. When the crust is done baking, remove it from the oven and carefully spread the PB&J mixture on top of the crust. Top with the chopped peanuts.
8. Bake the bars for 15 minutes. The jam mixture should be hot and bubbly. Let cool completely for at least 2 hours.
9. Remove from the pan and cut into 16 bars. Chill the bars overnight to help continue the solidifying process.

TIP: These bars turn out so much better when they have time to cool properly before they're chilled overnight in the refrigerator. Don't skip this step or you will just have a PB&J mash on your hands! I recommend wrapping them individually for the trail after the cooling time and then freezing them until you're ready to head out. They can be stored in the fridge for 3 to 4 days or in the freezer for up to a month.

CRISPY CILANTRO-LIME ROASTED CHICKPEAS

GLUTEN-FREE, NUT-FREE, VEGAN

SERVES 2 / PREP TIME: 40 MINUTES / COOK TIME: 45 MINUTES

This is an easy snack to have on the trail that is not only lightweight, but also packs in the protein to keep your energy up. I personally love the flavor of lime and cilantro together and they pair perfectly with the mild flavor of chickpeas.

1 (15 ounce) can chickpeas

1 tablespoon olive oil

½ teaspoon sea salt

½ teaspoon black pepper

3 tablespoons lime juice

1 tablespoon fresh cilantro, finely chopped

1. Strain the chickpeas and rinse them thoroughly. Lay the chickpeas out on a paper towel to dry for 30 minutes.

2. Remove any skins from the chickpeas (this helps the roasting process).

3. Preheat the oven to 425°F.

4. In a large bowl, combine the chickpeas, olive oil, salt, pepper, lime juice, and cilantro.

5. Pour the chickpea mixture onto the pan and space it out evenly into a single layer.

6. Bake for 40 to 50 minutes, stirring every 10 minutes until crispy.

7. Let cool and pack into a resealable plastic bag.

TIP: Chickpeas are also called garbanzo beans, which was confusing for me when I first started looking for them in the grocery store. It's also possible to use dried chickpeas instead of canned. Simply soak them overnight and then proceed with step 1 of the recipe.

HOMEMADE TRAIL CRACKERS

NUT-FREE, VEGETARIAN

SERVES 4 / PREP TIME: 10 MINUTES / COOK TIME: 9 MINUTES

I call these crackers but really they're glorified cookies. Which is fine, since a little sugar on the trail is usually what helps move feet along a little easier. The molasses in these gives them really full flavor so just a few go a long way!

7 tablespoons butter

½ cup brown sugar

½ cup white sugar

1 tablespoon molasses or honey

2 cups flour

1 teaspoon baking soda

1 teaspoon ground cinnamon

½ teaspoon salt

⅓ cup honey

2 teaspoons vanilla extract

3 tablespoons water

1. Preheat the oven to 350°F. Line a baking sheet with parchment paper.
2. Soften, but don't melt, the butter. About 10 seconds in the microwave is perfect.
3. In a stand mixer, cream the butter, brown sugar, white sugar and molasses at high speed for 3 to 4 minutes, or until creamy, scraping down the sides once.
4. In another bowl, mix the flour, baking soda, cinnamon, and salt until well mixed.
5. Add the dry ingredients to the wet ingredients and mix on medium speed with a paddle attachment for 2 minutes until well combined. The mixture will resemble coarse crumbs.
6. Add the honey, vanilla, and water and mix until the dough sticks together.

7. Form the dough into a ball. Lightly flour a surface and pat the dough onto the surface until about 2 inches thick. Carefully flip the dough so the flour is on the other side, too.
8. Roll the dough out to about ⅛ inch thick.
9. Cut out cracker shapes using a small cookie or biscuit cutter. I use one that is about 1 inch in diameter.
10. Bake for 7 to 9 minutes until the sides are slightly browned.
11. Let cool completely on the baking sheet.
12. Store in an airtight container for 5 days or in the freezer for 1 month.

TIP: You can make these crackers in any shape, but I like to make them bite-size for easy snacking on the trail. They also have less of a chance of crumbling when they are small.

MAPLE CINNAMON TRAIL MIX

DAIRY-FREE, GLUTEN-FREE, VEGAN

SERVES 6 / **PREP TIME:** 5 MINUTES / **COOK TIME:** 10 MINUTES

This trail mix is chock-full of protein with just enough sweetness to keep you satisfied and your energy levels high. It's good on its own, but it's also delicious with a little yogurt for breakfast or even with milk as a cold cereal.

1 cup pumpkin seeds

1 cup walnuts, chopped

1 cup raw almonds, whole, unsalted

1 teaspoon ground cinnamon

3 tablespoons maple syrup

1½ teaspoons salt

1 cup dried cranberries

1. Preheat the oven to 350°F.
2. In a large bowl, combine the pumpkin seeds, walnuts, almonds, cinnamon, maple syrup, and salt. Mix well.
3. Line a baking sheet with parchment paper and spread the trail mix on the paper. Bake for 10 minutes.
4. Once cool, add the dried cranberries and stir to combine.
5. Divide into individual baggies as needed for the trail.

STORAGE TIP: You can store this trail mix in an airtight container for up to 10 days before it starts to get stale.

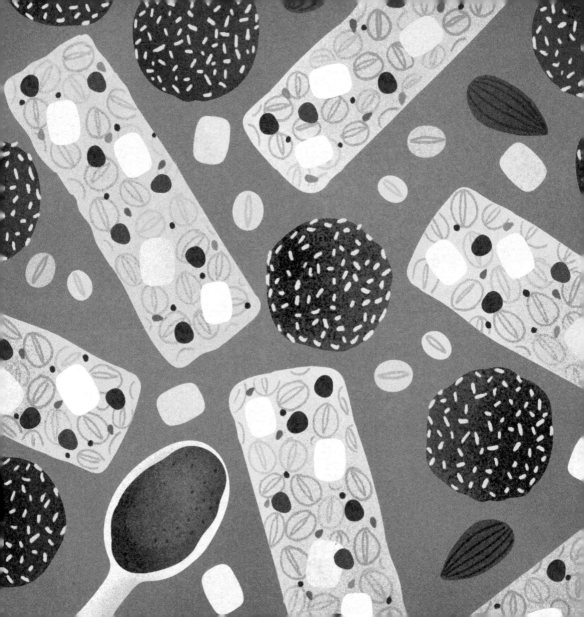

CHAPTER 10

BACKCOUNTRY DESSERTS AND DRINKS

Celebrate your accomplishments (yes, that even means finally getting everyone out on the trail!) with some backcountry-specific desserts and drinks. These recipes are meant to be easy to prepare, with many of them requiring just one pot. The goal is more sweet celebration and fewer dishes.

TRAIL APPLE CRISP

DAIRY-FREE, GLUTEN-FREE, VEGAN

SERVES 2 / PREP TIME: 10 MINUTES / COOK TIME: 15 MINUTES

This dessert is light to carry, easy to cook, and has just the right level of sweetness—not too much, not too little. So if you want a little something sweet but don't want to work too hard for it, this is your dessert!

1½ cups freeze-dried apples

3 tablespoons brown sugar

1 teaspoon ground cinnamon

¼ teaspoon ground cloves

6 tablespoons water

⅓ cup gluten-free granola

¼ cup chopped walnuts (optional)

PREP AT HOME

1. In a resealable plastic bag, add the freeze-dried apples, brown sugar, cinnamon, and cloves. Write "6 tablespoons of water" on the outside of the bag so you remember how much you will need.

2. In another bag, add the granola and walnuts (if using).

AT THE CAMPSITE

3. Add the apple mixture and the water to a pot over a camp stove. Cook over a medium flame until the apples have softened, the sugar has dissolved, and the mixture thickens slightly. Stir often and add a little more water if needed as it cooks. Remove from heat.

4. Sprinkle the granola and walnuts (if using) over the top and eat directly from the pot!

NO-BAKE BROWNIE BITES

DAIRY-FREE, GLUTEN-FREE, VEGETARIAN

SERVES 6 / PREP TIME: 10 MINUTES / SET TIME: 30 MINUTES

When you're burning calories like crazy on the trail, there's nothing better than a sweet treat that gives you great energy, too. This recipe is my favorite healthy dessert, backcountry or not. Packed with healthy ingredients, these bites really do taste like brownies!

1 cup tightly packed pitted dates

1 cup raw almonds

1 cup walnuts

⅓ cup cocoa powder

1 teaspoon pure vanilla extract

½ teaspoon sea salt

Unsweetened coconut flakes, for coating (optional)

1. Place the dates in a bowl and cover with enough hot water to submerge them. Soak for 15 minutes and then drain the water.

2. Place the almonds and walnuts in a food processor or blender and pulse until they are broken up into small pieces.

3. Add the dates, cocoa powder, vanilla, and salt and mix just until it forms a thick and sticky dough, making sure not to overmix.

4. Form the mixture into balls using about 1 tablespoon of dough per ball. Roll the balls in the coconut (if using), then place in the freezer to firm up, at least 30 minutes.

CHOCOLATE CHIP COOKIE BARS

NUT-FREE, VEGETARIAN

SERVES 2 TO 4 / PREP TIME: 10 MINUTES / COOK TIME: 15 MINUTES

I love to bring these cookie bars out on the trail. They're perfect for on-the-go snacks or after-dinner desserts. The whole-wheat flour makes them slightly nutty and also provides a boost of nutrition. And can you really go wrong with a cookie on the trail? I don't think so!

1 cup whole-wheat flour

1¼ cups white flour

1½ tablespoons ground flaxseed

1 teaspoon baking soda

1 teaspoon sea salt

2 teaspoons ground cinnamon (optional)

1 cup unsalted butter, softened

¾ cup packed brown sugar

2 eggs

1 tablespoon vanilla extract

1 cup dark chocolate chips

1. Preheat the oven to 375°F. Spray a 9-by-13-inch pan with nonstick cooking spray.

2. In a medium bowl, mix the flours, flaxseed, baking soda, salt, and cinnamon (if using). Set aside.

3. In a large bowl, cream together the butter and brown sugar until smooth, about 3 minutes.

4. Mix in the eggs and vanilla and stir with a spoon until just combined.

5. Add the dry ingredients slowly, mixing as you go to combine.

6. Add the chocolate chips and stir until just mixed in.

7. Spread the mixture evenly in the greased pan. Bake for 20 to 25 minutes or until golden brown. Cool in the pan and cut into bars.
8. Wrap individually to take as trail treats.

RASPBERRY DIRT PUDDING

NUT-FREE, VEGETARIAN

SERVES 2 / PREP TIME: 5 MINUTES / **SET TIME:** 1 HOUR

This delicious pudding takes a while to set, so plan to start this recipe right when you get into camp for so it's waiting for you when you're ready for dessert. The raspberries with the chocolate cookies and pudding is a match made in heaven.

½ cup freeze-dried raspberries

4 chocolate sandwich cookies, crushed

½ cup instant chocolate pudding mix (1 small box that says it serves 4 will work)

½ cup powdered whole milk

1 cup cold water

PREP AT HOME

1. In a resealable plastic bag, combine the raspberries and crushed cookies.

2. In a second bag, combine the pudding mix and powdered milk.

AT THE CAMPSITE

3. Add the cold water to the bag with the pudding mix.

4. Seal the bag and mix well by shaking and kneading it.

5. Let sit for at least 1 hour in a relatively cold spot (ideally a cooler, if you have one), preferably more, to let it thicken up.

6. Once the pudding is set up, top with the raspberry and cookie mixture. Split the dessert between two bowls and enjoy!

TIP: To cut down on waste and dishes, once I have added the toppings to the pudding, I just scoop half of the pudding back into the topping bag so each person has their own pudding bag to eat from.

CORNFLAKE ENERGY BARS

VEGAN

SERVES 2 TO 4 / PREP TIME: 10 MINUTES / SET TIME: 2½ HOURS

I'll be honest—because of the amazing chocolate topping, these are *not* the best option for hot temperatures in the backcountry. (Unless, of course, you're okay with being covered in melted chocolate.) They do, however, offer amazing energy for high-alpine adventures!

1 cup pitted dried dates

3 cups cornflake cereal, slightly crushed

½ cup shelled unsalted sunflower seeds

3 tablespoons coconut oil

⅓ cup dark chocolate chips

1. Line an 8-inch square baking dish with parchment paper.
2. Pulse the dried dates in a food processor or blender until it becomes a thick, sticky paste.
3. Transfer the dates to a large bowl and add the cornflakes, sunflower seeds, and coconut oil. Stir until well combined. Press the cornflake mixture into the bottom of the prepared baking dish.
4. Carefully melt the chocolate chips by microwaving in 30-second increments, mixing, then microwaving again until melted.

5. Pour the chocolate over the cornflake mixture, spreading evenly.
6. Let cool for about 20 minutes, then refrigerate for another 2 hours until firm.
7. Remove from the pan and cut into 12 bars.
8. Wrap each bar individually and store in an airtight container in the fridge for up to 2 months.

TIP: Though it's not required, a stand mixer works wonders for making the cornflake mixture easy to combine.

S'MORE GRANOLA BARS

DAIRY-FREE, VEGETARIAN

MAKES 9 BARS / PREP TIME: 10 MINUTES / COOK TIME: 20 MINUTES

Missing s'mores out in the backcountry? Look no further! These bars are just what you need to kick the craving and pack in some great energy at the same time. This is a great recipe for using up all those extra s'more ingredients just lying around. My family always seems to end up with a collection of broken crackers and half-eaten chocolate bars—this recipe is the way to use those up.

¼ cup chia seeds

12 pitted dried dates

¾ cup water

½ cup maple syrup

½ teaspoon salt

2¼ cups rolled oats

2 cups crushed graham crackers

½ cup mini marshmallows

½ cup dark chocolate chips (or 1 chocolate bar, chopped)

1. Preheat the oven to 350°F.

2. Mix the chia seeds, dates, water, maple syrup, and salt in a medium bowl and let soak for 10 minutes. Make sure the chia seeds are covered by water as they soak.

3. Put the mixture in a food processor or blender and process until smooth. Let cool slightly (about 5 minutes).

4. Put the mixture back in the bowl and add the oats, graham crackers, marshmallows, and chocolate chips. Mix until well combined.

5. Line a 9-inch square baking pan with parchment paper. Spread the mixture in the pan and press down hard with your palm to pack it down.

6. Bake for 20 minutes. Remove from oven and let cool completely before cutting into 9 bars.
7. Wrap each bar individually and store in an airtight container in the fridge for up to 2 months (though you'll never have them for that long!).

TIP: Don't have mini marshmallows on hand? Cut up some large ones into small cubes.

CHOCOLATE AND BANANA CHIP WRAPS

DAIRY-FREE, VEGETARIAN

SERVES 4 / PREP TIME: 10 MINUTES

Wraps are easy to hold, easy to eat, *and* keep well on the trail. The chocolate spread makes this recipe more of a dessert, but it can totally pass as an easy breakfast or snack, too.

⅓ cup chocolate hazelnut spread

4 tortillas or flatbread pieces

1 cup banana chips, divided

1. Layer the chocolate hazelnut spread evenly on one side of each of the tortillas.

2. Add ¼ cup of banana chips on top of the chocolate hazelnut spread.

3. Roll up and enjoy.

> **TIP:** This recipe uses banana chips since they are easier to haul than fresh bananas, but it doesn't mean you couldn't use fresh bananas at the beginning of your trip. It's also delicious with sliced fresh apples.

NO-BAKE CHOCOLATE CHEESECAKE

NUT-FREE, VEGETARIAN

SERVES 6 / **PREP TIME:** 10 MINUTES / **SET TIME:** 10 MINUTES

This is the ultimate treat for backpacking. It's certainly not healthy in any way, but it's something to look forward to after a long day on the trail.

20 chocolate
sandwich cookies

1 packet no-bake
cheesecake mix

2 tablespoons vegetable oil

1½ cups cold water

PREP AT HOME

1. Put the cookies in a resealable plastic bag along with about half of the crust crumbs from the no-bake cheesecake mix. Reserve the rest of the crust from the mix to use for something else (but make sure to date and label it).

2. Pack the cake mix in a separate resealable plastic bag.

AT THE CAMPSITE

3. Crush cookies into small crumbs. Slowly add a little oil to the bag and knead until it becomes moldable.

4. Press the crust into one large bowl or individual serving bowls.

CONTINUED>

5. Add the cold water to the bag with the cheese-
    cake mix, zip the top, and knead until blended.

6. Put the filling into the bowl (or bowls) and let set
    for about 10 minutes. Enjoy!

TIP: Feel free to reserve some of the crushed cookies
before adding oil to sprinkle on the top of the finished
dessert.

MEASUREMENT CONVERSIONS

OVEN TEMPERATURES

FAHRENHEIT	CELSIUS (APPROXIMATE)
250°F	120°C
300°F	150°C
325°F	165°C
350°F	180°C
375°F	190°C
400°F	200°C
425°F	220°C
450°F	230°C

WEIGHT EQUIVALENTS

US STANDARD	METRIC (APPROXIMATE)
½ ounce	15 g
1 ounce	30 g
2 ounces	60 g
4 ounces	115 g
8 ounces	225 g
12 ounces	340 g
16 ounces or 1 pound	455 g

VOLUME EQUIVALENTS

	US STANDARD	US STANDARD (OUNCES)	METRIC (APPROXIMATE)
LIQUID	2 tablespoons	1 fl. oz.	30 mL
	¼ cup	2 fl. oz.	60 mL
	½ cup	4 fl. oz.	120 mL
	1 cup	8 fl. oz.	240 mL
	1½ cups	12 fl. oz.	355 mL
	2 cups or 1 pint	16 fl. oz.	475 mL
	4 cups or 1 quart	32 fl. oz.	1 L
	1 gallon	128 fl. oz.	4 L
DRY	⅛ teaspoon	–	0.5 mL
	¼ teaspoon	–	1 mL
	½ teaspoon	–	2 mL
	¾ teaspoon	–	4 mL
	1 teaspoon	–	5 mL
	1 tablespoon	–	15 mL
	¼ cup	–	59 mL
	⅓ cup	–	79 mL
	½ cup	–	118 mL
	⅔ cup	–	156 mL
	¾ cup	–	177 mL
	1 cup	–	235 mL
	2 cups or 1 pint	–	475 mL
	3 cups	–	700 mL
	4 cups or 1 quart	–	1 L
	½ gallon	–	2 L
	1 gallon	–	4 L

INDEX

C

ACKNOWLEDGMENTS

When I signed on to write this book, I had no idea what life living through a pandemic was going to be like. I have to thank the Callisto team for all their patience as I suddenly juggled homeschooling my kids, keeping everyone sane at home, and testing recipes with limited resources at the grocery stores. It has certainly been an unforgettable experience.

A huge thanks to my TMM team who not only consistently helped me test recipes on the fly for their own outdoor families, but also gave me honest feedback (as usual) as I tweaked and changed them. I am so thankful for you every day.

And I can't forget my sweet family who gave me time to write in the midst of so much change and chaos. Bill, you inspire me daily to be a better mom, and I'm so thankful I chose you to be my adventure partner and the father of my children. Thank you for getting us out the door every day. Jack, Peter, Liza, Mara, and Nora, thank you for helping me test recipes. I love you more than you'll ever know.

ABOUT THE AUTHOR

AMELIA MAYER lives with her husband, five children, and one dog in Grand Teton National Park. She finds her sanity outdoors where the fresh air seems to dull any whining and lets everyone breathe just a little easier.

She loves to cook and does her best to spruce up camping dining with some meals that are reserved for those trips only, but is okay eating hot dogs when needed. (Because sometimes everyone just needs a hot dog.)

Beyond camping and cooking, Amelia loves to ski, hike, bike, and spend time making memories with her family.

You can find Amelia online at TalesofaMountainMama.com and on Instagram, Facebook, and Pinterest at **@mtnmamatales**.